Library of
Davidson College

ACTA UNIVERSITATIS UPSALIENSIS
Studia Anglistica Upsaliensia
28

Helga Drougge

The Significance of Congreve's *Incognita*

Uppsala 1976

Distributor:
Almqvist & Wiksell International
Stockholm

Doctoral dissertation at the University of Uppsala

ISSN 0562-2719
ISBN 91-554-0465-0

© Helga Drougge
Printed in Sweden 1976
by LiberTryck, Stockholm
Phototypesetting:
TEXTgruppen i uppsala ab

Quotations from *Incognita* are from *"Incognita" and "The Way of the World,"* ed. A. Norman Jeffares, and quotations from Congreve's plays are from *The Complete Plays of William Congreve*, ed. Herbert Davis. Otherwise, I have used old editions of old texts where I could get hold of them (and, where applicable, seventeenth-century English translations of French texts); and, where not, modern editions, as well as some second-hand quotations of rare texts from modern critical works. This means that some quotations have modernized spelling, others not.

Since it is customary to thank one's supervisor for his helpful and perceptive criticism, it is perhaps difficult to be believed sincere in doing so. I really do, however, most sincerely want to express my gratitude to Professor Gunnar Sorelius for exactly that, and also for his patience, which has been beyond the call of duty in the reading of various untidy drafts. A grant from the University of Stockholm enabled me to visit the British Museum, where the courtesy of the staff made it possible to get much read in a small compass of time.

Mr. Peter Malekin of Durham University is principally responsible for my getting round to writing this thesis, but its shortcomings are no fault of his.

Contents

I. Introduction 9
II. Background 11
    i. French Short Fiction 11
    ii. The Importance of the Romance 13
    iii. The Manner of Scarron in England 15
III. Style 21
    i. Some Features of Seventeenth-Century Narrative 21
    ii. The Facetious Style as Parody 28
    iii. The Self-Conscious Narrator 36
    iv. The Conciseness of Congreve 40
    v. "Rhetoric" 44
IV. Structure 47
    i. The Plot 47
    ii. Background 1: The World of Romance 51
    iii. Background 2: The Happy Mistake 55
    iv. Functionalism 58
    v. Facetious Structure 62
V. Parody 74
    i. Introduction 74
    ii. Restoration Parody 78
    iii. Literary Clichés 80
VI. *Incognita* and the Comedies 90
VII. Conclusion 96
Appendix: "The Preface to the Reader" 98
Bibliography 102
    i. Editions of *Incognita* 102
    ii. Other Primary Sources 102
    iii. Secondary Sources 103
Index 106

I. Introduction

Incognita was published in 1692,[1] when Congreve was twenty-two years old. The assertion in *Biographia Britannica* that it was actually written when he was only seventeen is widely quoted; but the tradition which this statement is based on is surely very likely to have some relation to the Augustan fashion for ascribing writings, wherever practically possible, to youth or even childhood, as Pope did. It is of a piece with the boastful pseudo-modesty of Congreve's Preface to *Incognita*, where he says that he is

> very well satisfy'd how much more proper it had been for [the reader] to have found out this [*Incognita*'s similarity to "dramatick writing"] himself, than for me to prepossess him with an Opinion of something extraordinary in an Essay began and finished in the idler hours of a fortnight's time: for I can only esteem it a laborious idleness, which is Parent to so inconsiderable a Birth.[2]

The reputation of the little book, at one time respectful if not enthusiastic, must have suffered considerably from the so-called abridged version by "the most ingenious Corinna" which was issued in 1730.[3] At least one critic, Gosse, quotes extensively from this version, apparently without being aware that it is not what Congreve wrote.[4] Not only does the ingenious Corinna save space by omitting the passages where Congreve "digresses"; she uses most of it up again in sentimental additions of compliments and celestial charms, and she ruins any joke she touches. It seems quite possible that this version was what literary historians and critics had read, up to the 1922 reprint of the original in the Percy Reprints;[5] and that it may, via the nineteenth-century critics, still colour the estimates of those later writers who are forced by the scope of their subjects to use some second-hand opinions. In any case, *Incognita* has turned out to be of little interest to writers of literary histories. Such attention as it

---

[1] Actually, it was "licensed on December 22, 1691, and was published by Peter Buck about two months later. It was advertised in the *London Gazette*, No. 2742, for the period from February 18 to February 22, 1691/2" (John C. Hodges, *William Congreve, the Man*, New York, 1941, p. 37, n. 13).

[2] *"Incognita" and "The Way of the World,"* ed. A. Norman Jeffares (London, 1966), p. 34. Page references to *Incognita* throughout are to this edition.

[3] It formed a part (Pt. 2, pp. 70–124) of the *Memoirs of the Life, Writings, and Amours of William Congreve Esq.* (London, 1730), supposedly written by Charles Wilson; cf. chapter VI below.

[4] Edmund Gosse, *Life of William Congreve* (London, 1888).

[5] *Incognita*, ed. H. F. B. Brett-Smith, The Percy Reprints, No. 5 (Oxford, 1922).

receives in these works is usually very complimentary, but there is not much of it. James Sutherland, for example, praises it enthusiastically, but his section of *The Oxford History of English Literature* deals with even such an oddity as Boyle's *Parthenissa* at greater length than *Incognita*.[6]

In some contexts it is natural to ignore the book. Maximillian E. Novak points out that *Incognita* "receives no attention whatever in works with titles like Ian Watt's *Rise of the Novel*, Francis Stoddard's *Evolution of the Novel*, Phelps' *Advance of the English Novel*, and Cross' *Development of the English Novel*."[7] This lack of interest is not surprising. As their titles indicate, these are evolutionary accounts of the history of fiction; a history which is regarded as consisting of a series of stages in a progress towards an end product. Such a conception means that a work of fiction must, in order to seem important, represent a step forward towards that end product; that is, it must be in some respect more like a modern or rather a late nineteenth-century realistic novel than the books which had been written before. It cannot accommodate a book like *Incognita*, which is conspicuously old-fashioned for its own time, and which seems like a throwback from the emerging realism of for example Aphra Behn to something not unlike the early version of Sidney's *Arcadia*. It would in fact be inappropriate to pay any attention to it in a "history of the novel" on these—traditional—premises.

There have been a few separate critical estimates, however, which display not merely non-committal benevolence but an active interest and appreciation. H. F. B. Brett-Smith's introduction to his edition in the Percy Reprints is sympathetic in spirit and very helpful about the background which conditioned *Incognita*. More recently, there has even been an instance of that extremely respectful and serious, almost theological, interpretation which has been such a popular approach to Restoration comedy.[8]

For my part, I found *Incognita* very charming and also teasingly odd, and I wanted to define just where its special quality lay. In making this attempt, I hope that I have illuminated some interesting trends in fiction at this, for fiction, highly interesting time: for I think that a great deal of the significance of *Incognita* lies in the unusually concentrated light it sheds on these trends. My more official aim, however, has been to try to show that in spite of the apparent discrepancy between manner and matter in it, *Incognita* is a single artistic whole, and a significant prologue to Congreve's plays.

---

[6] James Sutherland, *English Literature of the Late Seventeenth Century, Oxford History of English Literature*, VI (Oxford, 1969), 219.

[7] "Congreve's *Incognita* and the Art of the Novella," *Criticism*, 11 (1969), 329–42.

[8] Aubrey Williams, "Congreve's *Incognita* and the Contrivances of Providence," in *Imagined Worlds: Essays on Some English Novels and Novelists in Honour of John Butt*, ed. Maynard Mack and Ian Gregor (London, 1968), pp. 3–17; cf. IV:iii below.

II. Background

i. French Short Fiction

Charles C. Mish writes that "an account of English polite fiction during this period [1660—1700] reads like an echo, indistinct at times and with some teeth missing, of the French."[1] This was the classical period of French literature, and French culture was the big brother in the European family. Translations from the French dominated English publishing, and translations and unashamed and unacknowledged adaptations of French plays were popular pot-boilers on the stage; even the original English comedies were infiltrated by Frenchified fops. A background to Congreve's *Incognita* necessarily begins in France.

The short forms dominated French fiction completely in the classical period. The famous or notorious long romance—*le roman de longue haleine*[2] —had lost its hold on both readers and writers fairly abruptly around the year 1660. By then, the *précieux* perfect lovers and scrupulous mistresses were as old-fashioned as the prodigious heroes who slay ten thousand single-handed had become a generation before, or as the giants and enchanted castles in the generation before that (but cf. II:ii below). The machinery used for separating lovers—shipwrecks, pirates, incarcerations—handed down from the Alexandrian romances (cf. IV:ii below) had survived many centuries, but by 1660 it was generally ridiculed.[3]

After 1660, no single genre of prose fiction became as dominant as the romance had been earlier. Instead, there was a spectrum of genres, all comparatively short, some with short and well-defined periods of popularity (for example the fairy-tale in the nineties[4]), but most of them co-existing, developing and merging throughout the period and after. The most important genres were the "historical" and the "gallant" novel, which were not really two distinct

---

[1] Charles C. Mish, "English Short Fiction in the Seventeenth Century," *Studies in Short Fiction*, 6 (1969), 280 (I will refer to this useful work as "English Short Fiction" throughout).

[2] Maurice Magendie's *Le Roman français au XVIIe siècle* (Paris, 1932), which deals with the central thirty years of the genre, 1620—50, is an inexhaustibly concrete and illuminating account of the French seventeenth-century romance.

[3] By Charles Sorel in *De la connoissance des bons livres* (1671), for example; see IV:ii below.

[4] See Antoine Adam, *Histoire de la littérature française au XVIIe siècle*, V (Paris, 1956), 318—19.

kinds,[5] although the distinction is traditionally made by historians:[6] the historical novel was usually gallant as well and often centred round the revelation of the apocryphal secret amours of statesmen, while the gallant novel took over techniques for gaining conviction and local colour which had been developed by the writers of historical novels. The interest in atmosphere and setting came to the contemporary erotic novel via the historical erotic novel: one might call the gallant novel a historical novel with a setting which happens to be contemporary.[7] It is perhaps more convenient to use the terminology of Dorothy Dallas: she sees the "roman d'analyse" as the final, merged, version of both.[8]

The shift from romance to "roman d'analyse" was not only a shift from length to brevity but from the breathless piling-up of incidents to greater inwardness and simplicity, less "plottiness"; more psychology, fewer amazing coincidences and reversals. Du Plaisir points out in 1683 that the old romance and the new novel have the same aims: both try to please "par l'invention des incidents, par la constance des caractères, par la noblesse des pensées, par la justesse des mouvements du cœur." But the means they use to achieve these ends are very different:

> On ne cherche point aujourd'hui des incidents sur mer, ou dans la cour d'un tyran. L'action la plus légère peut former une action admirable, et tout l'art de faire valoir une petite circonstance, est de caractériser fortement, et d'une manière sensible, les personnes de qui on parle. Un homme dépeint avec tous les traits de la jalousie n'a pas besoin, pour avoir une douleur violente, de trouver sa maîtresse dans une conversation particulière avec un rival extraordinairement bien fait; la moindre civilité qu'elle lui rendra fera trembler le lecteur par la crainte que cette extrême jalousie ne produise quelque effet funeste. Une femme fière, et qui voudrait éternellement cacher sa faiblesse à un homme qu'elle aime, fera compatir les lecteurs lorsqu'elle sera au moindre danger de paraître devant lui; et ces divers mouvements de crainte ou de pitié pénétreront davantage dans nos cœurs, que quand nous voyons, ou un prince seul attaqué par un grand nombre d'ennemis, ou une princesse exposée sur le sable au flux des eaux, ou à la rencontre des bêtes farouches.[9]

At the same time, these new short forms had little in common with the older French novella tradition,[10] which had produced some remarkable works

---

[5] This is illustrated by the case of *La Princesse de Clèves*, which has been considered both the finest historical novel (by Antoine Adam) and the finest gallant novel (by B. A. Morrissette) of the period; see Mish, "English Short Fiction," p. 280, n. 88.

[6] See Antoine Adam, *Histoire de la littérature française au XVII*ᵉ *siècle*, IV (Paris, 1954), 172−77.

[7] Ibid., p. 177.

[8] Dorothy F. Dallas, *Le Roman français de 1660 à 1680* (Paris, 1932), pp. 93−167.

[9] *Sentiments sur les lettres et sur l'histoire, avec des scrupules sur le style*; quoted in Frédéric Deloffre, *La Nouvelle en France à l'âge classique* (Paris, 1967), p. 47.

[10] My account of this tradition relies on Deloffre, *La Nouvelle en France*, pp. 9 ff.

around the middle of the sixteenth century. The qualities incisively suggested by Du Plaisir in the passage I have quoted distinguished the novels of Mme de Villedieu and Mme de Lafayette not only from the long-winded romance, but even more sharply from the earlier short fiction in France. This short fiction had been, after the brilliant period around 1560, completely eclipsed by the romance for almost a century. It had been of the Italian type, inspired by the translations of Boccaccio and Bandello, that is to say "un récit assez bref, plaisant et volontiers grivois, ordinairement encadrée" (Deloffre, *La Nouvelle en France*, p. 19). The *encadrement*, whereby a collection of short novellas were enclosed in a "frame" story, as in *Decamerone*, was an almost universal feature of the genre; most of the tales in Marguerite of Navarre's *Heptaméron*, the best-known of the collections, were neither facetious nor indelicate, however. Featuring a complicated and sensational plot plainly and concisely told, this type of tale was known as a *nouvelle* up to the middle of the next century. In the decade 1660-70[11] this kind of story, with its drastic events compressed within the compass of a few pages, began to be called a *conte* instead. This is because the word *nouvelle* was needed, from 1660 onward, for a new major genre which may be called the Spanish kind of story, to continue the somewhat facile equation of geography and genre: compared to the *conte* it is longer, less "plotty," more "naive," more natural, with more atmosphere and local colour. The "roman d'analyse," a subtype of the *nouvelle*, soon became the dominant type. Adam sees this new psychological fiction, inaugurated by Segrais and reaching maturity in Mme de Lafayette's *Princesse de Monpensier* (1662), as a really new departure in literary history, despite the qualifications which always adhere to any such statement.[12] It was in this fiction that the spirit of the realistic part of Cervantes' *Novelas Ejemplares* (1612) was belatedly naturalized in French literature, although the collection had been translated and much admired as early as 1615.

ii. The Importance of the Romance

The influence of the romance on the emerging psychological fiction was at least as important as that of Cervantes, however. There is a direct line from the finely-drawn scrupulosities and amorous problems and discussions of la Calprenède and Mme de Scudéry to the erotic psychology of Mme de Lafayette. Moreover, the older, more martial and eventful type of romance,

---

[11] From the usage of La Fontaine, Deloffre concludes that it is during this decade that the transition takes place (*La Nouvelle en France*, p. 19).
[12] *Histoire de la littérature française au XVIIe siècle*, IV, 172-73.

laughed at and denounced as it was, remained to some extent the fixed star by which the later seventeenth-century writers of fiction oriented themselves, and defined their position. It may seem extraordinary that writers of the later seventeenth century should take so much trouble as they do to dissociate themselves from those who write about giants and captive maidens and heroes of supernatural prowess, since nobody, according to that official literary history which I have outlined above, actually wrote this kind of romance any longer. However, although it had disappeared from literary history as that discipline has traditionally been conceived—that is, from polite literature—it had not disappeared from the book-shops.[13] While nobody with cultural pretensions either wrote or confessed to reading chivalric romances in the seventeenth century, they remained extremely popular on other levels. The old romances like *Amadis* and *Palmerin* were reprinted throughout the century, in cheap editions and debased versions, and eventually in chap-books. To meet the demand, there was also a production of sub-literary new romances and new translations. Thus Du Verdier in France wrote new chivalric romances from 1626 onwards in great quantities,[14] and Anthony Munday in England "aided and abetted by various English publishers, started in this country a factory for the translation of chivalresque romances of foreign origin,"[15] which flourished around the year 1600.

This background explains why the serious writers of the late seventeenth century were still so very much aware of the romance: not as an alternative, but as a point of reference, something to dissociate themselves from. In blatant defiance of the actual facts, it remained something of a prefatorial commonplace to assume an attitude of lonely daring in eschewing the well-tried ornaments of the heroic romance: shipwrecks, letters, armings and devices.[16]

It gives a piquant perspective to note that this trick of dissociation was popular with the more sophisticated late romancers themselves, as well as with their novelistic successors (cf. IV:v and V:iii below): "But not to dress a true story in cloaths of a Romance," says Boyle's Artabanes, "I will pass by the description of our Arms, Devices, Motto's, and all things of so low a nature..."[17]

---

[13] See Louis B. Wright, *Middle-Class Culture in Elizabethan England* (Chapel Hill, N. Carolina, 1935), pp. 375 ff.

[14] Magendie, *Le Roman français*, pp. 173 ff.

[15] According to Professor Fitzmaurice-Kelly, quoted in Wright, *Middle-Class Culture*, p. 380.

[16] See for example *Prefaces to Four Seventeenth-Century Romances*, ed. Charles Davies, Augustan Reprint Society, No. 42 (Los Angeles, 1953).

[17] *Parthenissa* (London, 1676), Pt. I, Bk. 1, p. 8; cf. Thomas B. Haviland, *The Roman de Longue Haleine on English Soil* (Philadelphia, 1931), p. 118.

Congreve's definition of his own position in relation to the romance in the well-known Preface to *Incognita*, which I discuss in the Appendix, is consequently not very new or startling in 1692:

> Romances are generally composed of the Constant Loves and invincible Courages of Hero's, Heroins, Kings and Queens, Mortals of the first Rank, and so forth; where lofty Language, miraculous Contingencies and impossible Performances, elevate and surprize the Reader into a giddy Delight, which leaves him flat upon the Ground whenever he gives of, and vexes him to think how he has suffer'd himself to be pleased and transported, concern'd and afflicted at the several Passages which he has Read, *viz.* these Knights Success to their Damosels Misfortunes, and such like, when he is forced to be very well convinced that 'tis all a lye. Novels are of a more familiar nature; Come near us, and represent to us Intrigues in practice, delight us with Accidents and odd Events, but not such as are wholly unusual or unpresidented, such which not being so distant from our Belief bring also the pleasure nearer us. Romances give more of Wonder, Novels more Delight. (pp. 32—33)

Segrais had made a distinction between novel and romance thirty-five years earlier,[18] and since his distinction is an attempt to rescue fiction from the deadening *précieuse* demand for delicacy—*bienséance*—his emphasis is different from Congreve's. His position may be paraphrased as "romances give more of *bienséance*, novels more realism." Nevertheless, Congreve's distinction is hardly revolutionary in 1692. Superior references to invincible courages had been commonplace ever since the 1620's, when Camus[19] voiced his moral objections to the lies of the romance. Although the old romances were still being printed and read in 1692, then, only a very foreshortened perspective can make the Preface to *Incognita* look like a daring attack on contemporary conventions.

iii. The Manner of Scarron in England

In England, the first sixty years of the seventeenth century were a meagre period for prose fiction in general, not only for the short forms as in France.[20] There is a conspicuous falling-off after the brisk and interesting developments of the late sixteenth century, and only occasional and poor imitations of the older models—Greene, Lodge, Deloney—are produced. Old books provide the only native bestsellers in this period: *Arcadia, Euphues, Pandosto*.[21] Transla-

---

[18] In *Les Nouvelles françoises: ou Les Divertissemens de la princesse Aurelie* (Paris, 1656—57); see Appendix below.
[19] See Magendie, *Le Roman français*, pp. 140—41.
[20] See Mish, "English Short Fiction," pp. 233—79.
[21] See Charles C. Mish, "Best Sellers in Seventeenth-Century Fiction," *Papers of the Bibliographical Society of America,* 47 (1953), 356—73.

tions of important foreign works are of poor quality and appear long after the originals: *Decamerone* does not appear in English in a complete version until 1620. The *Novelas Ejemplares* of Cervantes are also translated very late, in 1640, and then only six of the original twelve tales are rendered. It is significant that the translator, James Mabbe, chooses the romantic, "plotty" tales, rather than the more original and realistic low-life ones (see p. 56 below): the achievement of Cervantes is unappreciated, as is also shown by the uncomprehendingly farcical way of reading *Don Quijote*, which was not discovered by serious readers at all, in contrast to the situation in France.[22]

I began this chapter by quoting Mish's words on the all-important French influence which led at any rate to a quantitative renaissance of prose fiction in the Restoration period: over four hundred titles were published between 1660 and 1700.[23] The important French fiction and much of the unimportant was enthusiastically translated and imitated in this period. The pseudo-historical French novels which I mentioned above were even more popular in England than in France, and the "facetious" French writers like Scarron and Furetière appealed immensely to the Restoration reader.[24]

In fact, it is difficult to escape the impression that the more transitory French fashions were imported into England with uncritical wholeheartedness, while the central and radical tendencies most worthily represented by Mme de Lafayette were less influential. To be sure, her work was translated (*Princess of Montpensier* in 1666, *Princess of Cleves* in 1679); but psychological fiction does not really arrive in England until Richardson. The only representative of realism, and that of a patchy kind, is Aphra Behn. Regarded as an echo of French fiction, which is what it is, Restoration prose fiction does have the most important teeth missing. The import which seems to have been most congenial of all to the temper of the English reading public is that of the facetious or "gay" (Boyce's term) novel. The jocular, self-deprecating way of telling a story, with a chattily intrusive narrator who comments on his story, draws parallels, "proves" that he is telling the truth, or admits that he does not know all the details of what happened, and in general talks to the reader, was first made fashionable in the Restoration period by the example of Scarron.[25]

---

[22] E. B. Knowles in his article "Cervantes and English Literature" (in *Cervantes across the Centuries*, ed. Angel Flores and M. J. Benardete, New York, 1947, pp. 267–93) traces this particular instance of backwardness to the uncordial political relations between Spain and England.

[23] Mish, "English Short Fiction," p. 279.

[24] Scarron's novels and his *Roman comique* were both translated in 1665, Furetière's *Roman bourgeois* in 1671 (under the title of *Scarron's City Romance*); see Charles C. Mish, *English Prose Fiction, 1600–1700: A Chronological Checklist* (Charlottesville, Virginia, 1967).

[25] See Mish, "English Short Fiction," p. 306.

Of course both burlesquely anti-romantic and more subtly self-deprecating stories had been written in England before the Restoration, too. The best example of the former is perhaps Nashe's *Unfortunate Traveller* (1594), and of the latter, Charleton's excellent little *Ephesian Matron* (1659). But the Restoration flood of self-conscious jocularity is a separate phenomenon. Technically, *The Ephesian Matron* has much in common with this vogue, and it is necessary to say a few words about it, although I certainly cannot do justice to its qualities in this brief survey.

Charleton's version of Petronius' story about the sorrowing widow who withdraws into her husband's tomb to die, but is reclaimed to life and happiness by the charms of a soldier who finds her there, is a celebration of physical love and an explicit attack on the fashionable distinctions between lust and love made by "the platonique sect." Many features of the story reappear in the later intrusive narrators: the mock-ignorance of what really happened, eked out with pseudo-helpful guesswork (cf. III:i—iii below), the learned digressiveness, the sardonic tone. Charleton specializes in medical and physiological paraphernalia, explaining for instance the absolutely ordinary effects of wine or love on his heroine in terms of a complicated machinery of vital spirits and subtle vapours. He is capable of employing ten pages of dialectic about Galen, atoms, and the distinction between the "*Rational*, or *Intellectual*" soul, and the "onely *Sensitive*" one[26] to refute the imaginary argument of a hypothetical "witty Disciple of *Epicurus*" (p. 34) that the mellowing effect of a draught of wine upon the widow's grief constitutes evidence against the immortality of the soul.

This has more of the real spirit of Scarron than the later self-styled "manner of Scarron" of the Restoration. Scarron, like Charleton, had used old stories which he retold in a personal way in his *Nouvelles tragicomiques tournées de l'espagnol en français* (1655—56). These were translated into English in 1665, together with three incidental "histories" from the *Roman comique*, under the title of *Scarron's Novels*. The urbanely intrusive style in which he retold his Spanish originals struck the English fancy very much. There was a vogue of more or less successfully humorous and ironic narrators[27] (mostly less), and Congreve's *Incognita* is part of the vogue. It seems illuminating to place the book in such a perspective, although this is not usually done by critics[28] who

---

[26] *The Ephesian Matron* (London 1659), p. 38.

[27] The vogue is surveyed in Mish's "English Short Fiction," pp. 306—16, and in the introductory notes in his anthology *Restoration Prose Fiction* (Lincoln, 1970), which reprints several examples of this fiction, such as *The Cimmerian Matron* (1668) and Kepple's *Maiden-Head Lost by Moon-Light* (1672).

[28] But compare B. Boyce, "The Effect of the Restoration on Prose Fiction," *Tennessee Studies in Literature*, 6 (1961), 77—83.

discuss the lightly bantering tone in which the story is told; naturally enough, since most of this literature is deservedly little known today.

The English version of the manner of Scarron is much cruder than Scarron's own delightful colouring of his "translations" from the Spanish. There is something of the same unequal relation between French original and English copy as in the case of the other fashion started in England by the example of Scarron: the "travesties" of classical subjects in the wake of his *Virgile travesti* (1648).[29] The name of Scarron was quite unfairly associated with brutally self-indulgent burlesque writing in England, and the first of the fashionable brood of travesties both used and reinforced this tendency by its title: it was Cotton's *Scarronides* (1664). The English idea of what was typical of Scarron was probably more coloured by the *Roman comique* than by his short novels, and perhaps also by the ascription of Furetière's unsubtle *Roman bourgeois* (1666) to Scarron by an enterprising translator: it was published as *Scarron's City Romance* in 1671. At any rate, none of the self-consciously facetious English writers of the Restoration period approach the wit and sophistication of Scarron's novels. At its simplest, and most common, the fashionable facetiousness consisted merely of a monotonously jocular reader-nudging which is as irritating as Euphuism itself, and of an incontinent dribbling of exclamation marks and the word "well" over the page. Thus self-consciousness in the worst sense of the word is exhibited in the free 1673 translation of Le Pays' *Zelotyde* (1664):[30]

... the Spring had with her natural Artifice, (that you will say now is a strange one I hope) painted all the Trees and Meadows with her invisible Pencil ...[31]

Hardly more amusing is Aphra Behn's *The Court of the King of Bantam*,[32] which is a particularly significant example of "the manner of Scarron" in England, since it is supposed to represent a deliberate attempt by Aphra Behn to show that she could write like Scarron if she chose.[33] This ambition of hers manifests itself as a nervous exclamatoriness and a sprinkling of supposedly racy asides, like the parenthesis in her description of the morning after the evening upon which Mr. Would-be King has finally been admitted to the bed of his adored:

---

[29] See Sturgis E. Leavitt, "Paul Scarron and English Travesty," *SP*, 16 (1919), 108–20; cf. V:ii below.

[30] But cf. Boyce's description of it as the best "gay novel" before *Incognita*, in "The Effect of the Restoration."

[31] *The Drudge: or The Jealous Extravagant* (London, 1673), pp. 19–20. For Le Pays, the original *bel esprit*, see Dallas, *Le Roman français*, pp. 100–104.

[32] Published in 1696, but according to George Woodcock (*The Incomparable Aphra*, London, 1948, pp. 166–67) probably written before 1685.

[33] Woodcock, *The Incomparable Aphra*, p. 167.

The next Morning before the Titular King was (I won't say up, or stirring, but) out of Bed . . .[34]

The plot is a perfect match for this tone: it describes, with great gusto, the sexual and economic gulling of a conceited fool.

The fashion was still flourishing in 1692, when *Incognita* was published; quantitatively more so than ever, since the short novelettes which appeared monthly in Peter Motteux' *Gentleman's Journal* (1692—94) were of this type. Mish's description of Motteux' stories is more or less applicable to the whole school of "facetious" story-telling, with the single exception of *Incognita*:

. . . they are sex-stories rather than love-stories. The relations between men and women are looked at in a way that is, if not cynical, at least unromantic. In a word, these are fabliaux for those with some taste and education, and they necessarily involve some depiction of manners and a realistic viewpoint.[35]

Some taste and education, yes, but not very much. Motteux relies heavily on snobbery and on the laugh-raising capacity of heartless practical jokes and humiliations. The journalism of the nineties, of which Tom Brown and Ned Ward are the best-known representatives, along with Motteux himself, is not quite distinct from this kind of "comic" story-telling. The line between fiction and journalism, in a more or less modern sense, is very indistinct in their writings. Motteux' *Gentleman's Journal* itself has a sort of run-on technique which links the "novels," as the novelettes are called, with the rest of the contents of the issue.[36] This linking makes the self-conscious, intrusive style of his stories natural and almost unavoidable: each issue is a whole, and the chatty voice of the author is what keeps it together. Motteux talks to the reader, intimately, banteringly, very personally, from the first page to the last, and this is surely one of the reasons for the success of his *Journal*. The same voice keeps right on through the "novels," and goes on without a break into a poem or an essay on perpetuum mobile. Conversely, little gouts of fiction, anecdotes, are always breaking out in Ned Ward's *London Spy* (1698—1700). In the *Spy* as a whole, the anglicized manner of Scarron seems to have combined with the native tradition of scurrilous journalism[37] to produce the tiresome vivaciousness and the unflagging "comic similitudes" which characterize Ward's style. Such facetiousness, inextricably bound up with the snobbery and sadism which these early journalists themselves probably considered very racy and colour-

---

[34] *Works*, ed. Montague Summers (London, 1915), V, 32.

[35] "English Short Fiction," p. 314.

[36] See R. N. Cunningham, *Peter Anthony Motteux 1663—1718: A Biographical and Critical Study* (Oxford, 1933), p. 26.

[37] See Louis B. Wright, *Middle-Class Culture in Elizabethan England* (Chapel Hill, N. Carolina, 1935), pp. 435 ff.

ful, is very distant from the delicate balance of Congreve's style. Nevertheless the two belong together, at least in that the fashion for a jocular nudging of the reader, which was at its height in the nineties, is a necessary background for *Incognita*.

III. Style

i. Some Features of Seventeenth-Century Narrative

Incognita is a Scarronian novel only in the same sense as Sidney's *Arcadia* is a Heliodorean romance,[1] or *Hamlet* a revenge play; it is what the author has done with the category that matters. Nevertheless it is both logical and often illuminating to start with the category; that is, to start by considering *Incognita* as forming part of the facetious vogue.

To identify the leading characteristics of this fashionable style in which Congreve works it is necessary to retreat yet another step from the particular to the general and pay some attention to late seventeenth-century narrative technique in general. The serious English fiction of the period is in the main deservedly despised and unread today (except *The Pilgrim's Progress*), and therefore the features which are *not* peculiar to the facetious writer, but shared by all his contemporaries, may seem quirky or deliberately outrageous to a modern reader, without originally having been so in the least.

A striking example of such a feature is the so-called intrusiveness of the comic writers. It is only an exaggeration, and not a violent one, of the normal seventeenth-century way of telling a story. The intrusive narrator is not a "device" in the seventeenth century, since the non-intrusive, neutral narrator had not yet been invented. The disappearance of the narrator in his capacity as commentator and moralizer is a late, sophisticated idea, not merely in the criticism of fiction, which was still very undeveloped in the seventeenth century, but in fiction itself, too. Of course there were degrees of intrusiveness: the more ambitious and literary a text was, the more was the narrative material amplified by moralizing comments and learned allusions. Stories, being usually borrowed, were not considered much in themselves: the taste and genius of a writer were to be displayed in improving moral asides and apt classical parallels. Thus Du Plaisir (cf. II:i above), writing in 1683, saw the reflexions and thoughts of the writer as the crowning beauty of a story, and as the appropriate field for the display of talent and insight; only authors who lacked these advantages should confine themselves to the easier art of writing unadorned stories:

---

[1] See Samuel Lee Wolff, *The Greek Romances in Elizabethan Prose Fiction* (New York, 1912), pp. 307 ff.

Ceux qui ne se sentent point ces avantages, et qui d'ailleurs ont quelque disposition à écrire, doivent s'attacher seulement à l'histoire véritable, parce que l'on s'y contente davantage d'une vérité toute nue, et seulement embellie par l'ordre des matières, par la noblesse des expressions, et par l'exactitude du style; ou, si l'on veut entreprendre une nouvelle, il me paraîtrait raisonnable d'imaginer seulement et de réciter les faits, de trouver les événements naturels, de peindre les caractères, enfin d'écrire et de faire parler d'une manière noble, sans entrer dans aucunes réflexions parce que rien n'est plus désagréable qu'une pensée fausse, et peu juste.[2]

The fashion for such ornaments had started in France with Yver's *Printemps* (1572), the earlier French stories such as the *Heptaméron* being too short to accommodate much commentary. But neither these earlier stories nor the short and unambitious seventeenth-century fiction ever aimed at being neutral, at letting the reader react to the events of the story without the guidance of the author's moralizing commentary.

Nor can the concept of "point of view" be applied to this early fiction; a concept which is central in the modern analysis of fictional techniques.[3] The adoption of a point of view means that the narrator has eschewed omniscience in order to stay within the consciousness of one particular character throughout the story. Such sophisticated self-restraint would, to most earlier writers, have appearad to be wanton self-sacrifice. To renounce a whole spectrum of inviting possibilities "merely to make a story sound as if such and such a character was actually telling it"[4] necessarily seemed a bad bargain before its unexpected and sophisticated advantages had been explored. The unambitious and subliterary fiction, then, employed an omniscient and chattily intrusive narrator from mere helplessness, because that is the easiest and most primitive way to write a story; while the ambitious texts used a narrator even more obviously possessed of these same characteristics, because intrusions and excursions provided opportunities to display skill and erudition.

The normal way of writing was thus uninhibitedly intrusive: it was the way an unsophisticated writer could write without being conscious of writing in any particular way at all. It was the invisible style of the period, just as the invisible style of the twentieth century is that which assumes the point of view of one of the characters (or of one character at a time) in the story. Such a style could be used in ways that were as sophisticated as any of the modern forms of self-imposed restraint on the part of the narrator; to a writer who wished to write in a particular way, rather than "invisibly," the possible

---

[2] Quoted in Deloffre, *La Nouvelle en France*, p. 49.
[3] As developed by later critics, particularly Percy Lubbock; see p. 32 below.
[4] The phrase is Charles Muscatine's, *Chaucer and the French Tradition* (Berkeley, 1957), p. 172.

variations from the norm were rich and varied. Omniscience and commentary could be eschewed momentarily, for particular effects, although there was no question of consistently doing without them.

Aphra Behn provides examples of such variations from the seventeenth-century norm, being sometimes confidential and explicatory, sometimes withdrawn. Her memorable story *The Fair Jilt* (1688) may illustrate this. It is an account of crime and passion, and Aphra Behn assures the readers that it is all true. The fair jilt herself, Miranda, is a beautiful young woman of quality and fortune in Antwerp, "naturally amorous, but extremely inconstant,"[5] much followed and a great flirt. She falls passionately in love with a young friar (in fact a German prince with a tragic love story behind him) and is enraged when he repels her immodest advances. She accuses him of raping her, and he languishes in prison throughout the two years taken up by the rest of the story. Then Miranda falls in love with Prince Tarquin of Rome, perhaps especially with his title and quality, and he on his side is deeply in love with her. They get married, and live in such magnificent state as necessitates great inroads into the fortune of Miranda's young sister Alcidiana, to whom Prince Tarquin is guardian. When Alcidiana demands her portion, Miranda inveigles a young servant to try to murder her. She survives, however; the would-be murderer confesses all, and Miranda is sentenced to stand by the gibbet upon which he is hanged. She then persuades her husband to try to kill Alcidiana, but he too fails and is taken in the attempt. He is sentenced to death, but in the dramatic final scene, he miraculously escapes execution: the executioner strikes him in the shoulders instead of the neck, and the sympathetic people, who think Miranda the real criminal, carry him off to sanctuary. At long last, Miranda is penitent about the fate she has brought on her husband, and they go off and live privately in Holland.

These thrilling events are certainly not narrated in a neutral way, as a rule. Usually, Aphra Behn does not trust the reader to respond properly without her guidance: she prompts his reactions at every turn, telling him whom to pity and whom to abhor. Before she even begins to tell the story she provides a prescription of the suitable moral and emotional reaction to the story as a whole, and an interpretation of its meaning. Two pages of general reflexions on the different effects of love on different people are devoted to elucidating the moral to be drawn from the coming narrative:[6]

---

[5] *The Works of Aphra Behn*, ed. Montague Summers (London, 1915), V, 77.

[6] Mish describes this as "a gambit greatly favored by a number of French writers of the time: the story is said to be an illustration of some sententious amorous truth. Though these maxims are usually rather vague and general, the story itself never seems a very apt example of the principle stated" ("English Short Fiction," p. 303, n. 129).

> How far distant Passions may be from one another, I shall be able to make appear in these following Rules. I'll prove to you the strong Effects of Love in some unguarded and ungovern'd Hearts; where it rages beyond the Inspirations of *a God all soft and gentle,* and reigns more like *a Fury from Hell.* (p. 74)

The emphatic didacticism which is expressed here dominates most of Aphra Behn's stories; but there are also occasional understatements and withdrawals of the helpful narrator, which can be extremely effective. The final sentence of *The Fair Jilt* has been admired for its restraint:[7]

> Since I began this Relation, I heard that Prince *Tarquin,* dy'd about three Quarters of a Year ago. (p. 124)

The discretion and absence of commentary of this curtain-line form a striking contrast to the opening of the story. Such qualities exist only at certain moments, and for particular effects, in seventeenth-century fiction: the logic of the story as a whole is, at best, an artistic logic.

The same principle applies to the omniscience of the narrator. The narrator of *The Fair Jilt* usually looks effortlessly into the minds of her characters, but occasionally she has no idea what the motives of their actions may be, and tries to supplement her ignorance with guesswork. Not only that; she sometimes does not even know exactly what happened, and may suddenly be seen to be making use of incomplete notes taken at the time of the events described,[8] as when the law officers demand Alcidiana's portion:

> The Officer received for Answer, That the Money should be call'd in, and paid in such a Time, setting a certain Time, which I have not been so curious as to retain, or put in my Journal-Observations; but I am sure it was not long, as may be easily imagin'd, For they every Moment suspected the Prince would pack up, and be gone, some time or other, on the sudden. (pp. 109–10)

Of course the effect aimed at by such stratagems is one of realism: events appear to be related by a real person, who knows about them from ordinary fallible human sources. This, Aphra Behn insinuates, is not a "golden world" of the imagination, created by the author and completely available to inspection: it is the world itself, reality itself. In the passage quoted, she emphasizes and adds further conviction to the limitations of her source, the incomplete "Journal-Observations," by doing her best, with the help of such information as she has, to provide a reasonable approximation of the missing detail concerning the exact length of the time limit: "not long."

This is not the place for an exhaustive analysis of the realistic devices used

---

[7] See Mish, "English Short Fiction," p. 305.

[8] Cf. Maximillian E. Novak, "Congreve's *Incognita* and the Art of the Novella," *Criticism,* 11 (1969), 331.

by Aphra Behn.⁹ She is a pioneer of realism; she insists that "every Circumstance, to a Tittle, is Truth" (*The Fair Jilt*, p. 74), that she saw what happened with her own eyes. Nevertheless, while at pains to give this impression, she thinks nothing of dropping the momentary limitations in the sources of the narrator in favour of entering into the minds and feelings of the people she writes about, as if the "Journal-Observations" had never been mentioned:

> Unawares, unknown, and unwillingly, he gave her Wounds, and the Difficulty of her Cure made her rage the more: She burnt, she languish'd, and died for the young Innocent, who knew not he was the Author of so much Mischief.
> Now she resolves a thousand Ways in her tortur'd Mind, to let him know her Anguish, and at last pitch'd upon that of writing to him soft Billets . . . (p. 87)

Where is now the narrator who was glimpsed, in the passage quoted earlier, laboriously compiling a truthful account from limited sources? She now knows exactly what goes on inside her heroine. Consistency is sacrificed to what she wants to tell, as it is on every page; except that it is hardly right to call it a sacrifice. She is not interested in consistency of this merely logical nature. As far as logic is concerned, the effect of the moment is all.

This may almost be called the governing principle of seventeenth-century narrative technique. It governs comic fiction as well, of course: the facetious narrators are as elusive and inconsistent as the serious ones. This means that it is necessary to be careful when speaking of "narrators" at all in seventeenth-century fiction: in the logic-obsessed twentieth-century sense, there are no narrators. In other words, it is anachronistic to look for the popular modern technique of consistently differentiating the actual author from a fictitious, dramatized narrator, to whom the attitude of the author is ironical; while irony towards a narrator *of the moment* was a very popular and versatile comic and satiric device. This meant that the traits of the mask in front of the author's face changed, or the mask dropped, as required. Of course the great example of this technique is *A Tale of a Tub*, were Swift uses, from moment to moment, the *persona* which best answers the needs of that particular moment.¹⁰

In *Incognita*, there are glimpses of an appealingly featherbrained but splendidly poised, sardonic yet friendly character who is ostensibly telling the story:

---

⁹ A really insiduous refinement, reminiscent of twentieth-century journalistic techniques, occurs in *The Dumb Virgin* (1687), the events of which the author is supposed to have witnessed and to some extent partaken in herself: there is a character in it who calls himself Dangerfield, "which was a Name that so pleas'd me, that being since satisfied it was a Counterfeit, I us'd it in a Comedy of mine" (*Works*, V, 429). Thus she identifies herself as a producer of "literature"—in fact as the well-known contemporary figure Mrs. Behn, writer of comedies—which "literature" is effortlessly put on a different plane from, and contrasted with, this true account of the man who called himself Dangerfield.

¹⁰ F. R. Leavis analyses this aspect of *A Tale of a Tub* in "The Irony of Swift," in *The Common Pursuit* (1952; rpt. New York, 1964), pp. 73–87.

of a "narrator," or of the human face of Congreve; or perhaps of Congreve as he liked to picture himself; or the human face and voice which Congreve wanted to dramatize and present as a picture of himself because it was a suitable element in the kind of book he wanted to write. I have made it clear, I hope, that there is no point in worrying at these alternatives, and still less in speculating about whether he is being becomingly self-ironical in those passages where the voice becomes obviously foolish, and emphasizes its own foolishness; or whether he is not rather being ironical at the expense of a "narrator" he does not identify himself with. Such questions simply do not apply, because the facetious or ironic narrator here is of the same discontinuous nature as the serious narrator in *The Fair Jilt*, and he is equally incapable of being dramatized as a person distinct from the "author." If the narrators of Congreve and Charleton seem more substantial than those of Aphra Behn, it is because the contradictory glimpses we get of these characters are more elaborate and colourful than hers. All these narrators belong recognizably to the same family, however. The conscientious narrator poring over incomplete sources who was employed by Aphra Behn to make her story more realistically convincing can be recognized, in a comically heightened form, in Charleton's learned speculations in *The Ephesian Matron*. Charleton's narrator professes ignorance of what is the matter with his heroine, puzzledly describing all the time-honoured symptoms of love which are immediately recognized as such by the reader: the blush, the trembling lips, and so on. What, he asks himself, can it all mean? In an attempt to answer this question, he brings into play a wealth of physiological analysis and plodding logical deduction, without making much headway, until fortunately the Gordian knot is cut for him by the march of events, "for, behold, she now throws her self into the Souldier's arms" (p. 51). This dense but learned storyteller would certainly be incapable of the extremely intelligent and sharpsighted psychological perceptions which characterize Charleton's narrator on other pages of the story. He is obviously related to the delightful chinese-box narrators of *Don Quijote*,[11] and was presumably[12] influenced by them.

Congreve's narrator, then, is absolutely normal in being discontinuous and contingent upon the requirements of various comic or ironic effects. It would be anachronistic to expect anything else; and since this is so his scattiness only

---

[11] For an account of Cervantes' learned and inconsequential narrators, see Wayne C. Booth, "The Self-Conscious Narrator in Comic Fiction Before *Tristram Shandy*," *PMLA*, 67 (1952), 163–85.
[12] There is a reference to *Don Quijote* in *The Ephesian Matron*, in the form of the reflexion that "who can but fall into a rapture, in thinking of the vertues of Wine, or forbear to repeat father *Sancho*'s prayer that *Providence would never suffer him to want good store of that c[e]lestical Nectar*" (p. 34).

deserves a brief illustration. It is easy to contradict any definite statement about the personality and point of view of Congreve's narrator which can be extracted from quotations, by choosing a different set of quotations. Sometimes he relies upon second-hand information, apparently, since he does not even know everything that a man watching the scene would see:

... which Aurelian understanding, groped for the Knots, and either untied them or cut them asunder; ... (p. 72)

But in such cases he is very conscientious, and does his best to provide as much information as possible, for instance working out the missing fact here by using his brain:

but 'tis more probable the latter, because more expeditious.

On the other hand, he is omniscient and can enter into the characters' minds at will:

While several Conjectures pass'd among the Company, who were all gone to Dinner at the Palace, who those Cavaliers should be, Don Fabio thought himself the only Man able to guess; for he knew for certain that his Son and Hippolito were both in Town, and was well enough pleased with his humour of remaining Incognito till the Diversions should be over ... (p. 65)

Nonchalantly enough, however, he often quite deliberately refuses to tell all he knows, either because he pretends that he cannot do justice to a topic, a sudden access of modesty which is intended to tease rather than to excuse:

I should by right now describe her Dress, which was extreamly agreeable and rich, but 'tis possible I might err in some material Pin or other, in the sticking of which may be the whole grace of the Drapery depended. (pp. 43–44; cf. IV:iv below)

Or else for no reason at all, except to stress that he is the one who is in charge, even perversely pointing out that he is skipping something rather good:

He made her a very Passionate and Eloquent Speech in behalf of himself (much better than I intend to insert here) ... (p. 75)

Ignorant but ploddingly eager to oblige, or omniscient but teasingly selective: the demonstration need not be prolonged. To try to catch and dissect the personality of this appealing shadow would obviously be misguided,[13] for in

---

[13] But cf. Maximillian E. Novak's opinion that Congreve's narrator is an advance on that of Scarron, because Scarron "failed to make the narrator a believable and sympathetic character within the work," whereas "Congreve, like Fielding, attempted to introduce his personality into fiction, to drop his cynical stance when his emotions were engaged and without destroying the integrity of his fictional characters and their story, participate in their feelings and sensations. His narrator gives the impression of a man who has observed society, accepts its codes, understands all there is to understand about love, but believes in romantic love even though he understands just how silly it is" ("Congreve's *Incognita* and the Art of the Novella," *Criticism*, 11, 1969, 339).

spite of the "I" and the glimpses of a mocking personality which assumes a semblance of substance for a moment every now and then, this technique has nothing in common with that of dramatic monologue.

But there are further reasons for the luxuriant inconsistency of Congreve's narrator, besides his generic, "normal" lack of substance. The mocking, self-conscious tone of the best facetious writers, like Congreve and Charleton, did not depend on mere vague jocularity and general reader-baiting, as it often did in the poor writers. Instead, the comic effects of *Incognita* are parodies of corresponding "serious" effects in contemporary non-comic fiction.

ii. The Facetious Style as Parody

In his article "*Préciosité* and the Restoration Comedy of Manners,"[14] David S. Berkeley makes use of the terminology which George Orwell had developed to deal with comic postcards:[15] that of the official "soul"—the romantic view of marriage—versus the unofficial protest or "body"—the postcard world of mothers-in-law and shrill wives, a world which only has meaning, only is funny, if we know about its "soul."

Berkeley applies this pattern to Restoration comedy, which he sees as the unofficial view of the *précieuse* art of love. (In other words, he has added Orwell's terminology to Kathleen Lynch's incisive analysis of the significance of Restoration comedy.[16]) When the laws of *préciosité* are forgotten, as they are now, what was pointed and precise in the comedies becomes vague.

This terminology is useful for my purposes too: the "soul" of Restoration comic fiction is Restoration fiction in general, especially of course the new and trendy features of the most fashionable and conspicuous fiction. The fact that the "serious" fiction of the seventeenth century is little known today blurs the delights of that comic fiction which assumed that its readers were familiar with the romances and with the beginnings of the realistic novel. Moreover, the writers who exploited contemporary fictional conventions for comic purposes did so in a parody which is as fragmentary and discontinuous as other aspects of seventeenth-century narrative technique. This is another bar to modern understanding and appreciation, but the most formidable obstacle is certainly the historic accident that the "soul" of this parody is unfamiliar now. Fortunately it is neither necessary nor possible to make a comprehensive analysis of seventeenth-century fictional techniques here: I only want to point

---

[14] *Huntington Library Quarterly*, 18 (1955), 109–28.

[15] "The Art of Donald McGill" (1941), in *Decline of the English Murder and Other Essays* (Harmondsworth: Penguin Books, 1965), pp. 142–54.

[16] Kathleen M. Lynch, *The Social Mode of Restoration Comedy* (New York, 1926).

out in a very general way some of the more obvious changes that were taking place at the time of Congreve's *Incognita*. The trouble is that the parody of these changes was intended to be grasped immediately and intuitively by readers who had the correct frame of reference effortlessly present in their minds: it is impossible to do justice to it in the cumbersome explanations which are now needed to collect all the threads which lead to a single point.

Naturally enough, the comic writers of the seventeenth century did not parody contemporary fiction from a twentieth-century point of view. In other words, they did not necessarily choose those aspects of the "soul" which we would expect: it is not the old-established and universal inconsistencies, which are absurd to us, that are parodied, but more often the new attempts to write with less inconsistency, more realistically. From a present-day perspective these attempts are inconspicuous to the point of invisibility; nevertheless, they were real and important. There was actually a changing attitude, a growing awareness that some kind of limitation of the point of view, if only in the simplest physical sense, will make a story in some ways more convincing, more like something that has really happened.

To try to make a story realistic by claiming that it is factually true, that I myself, *moi qui vous parle*, was a witness, is perhaps philosophically not a very attractive method. The major novelists in France did not make any such claims: on the contrary, they often took pains to point out, and boast of, the artificiality of their product. Nevertheless, they employed their greatest skill —"artificiality," in seventeenth-century language—in trying to write *as if* the story might have actually happened, in producing an effect of *vraisemblance*.

Whether a story was meant actually to fool the readers, or only to make them suspend their disbelief, it was helpful to have the story told by somebody who was supposed to have found out its events in some reasonably credible way, like Aphra Behn's momentary narrator with his Journal-Observations. A particularly obvious case for this was that of the so-called "histories" in the long romances. These were stories which characters in the romance told each other; not just "stories" like Sheherazade's entertainment, but purportedly true accounts, usually the account of the teller's own life. They were very common in the romances, and they usually formed separate and quite detachable and self-contained stories; occasionally, in fact, they *were* detached and printed separately by an enterprising translator or printer.[17] But it was in their original context that the "histories" were particularly liable to offend the sense of *vraisemblance* of readers and carping critics (see below), because in the

---

[17] As in the case of the three "novels"—short stories—from Scarron's *Roman comique*, which were printed together with his "Spanish" novels as *Scarron's Novels* (translated by John Davies, 1665).

romance they had a narrator who was really and unmistakably distinct from the shadowy omniscient figure of the author, since the narrator was himself a character in the romance proper, and his audience were on the inside too. The "history" had to be appropriate to the person who told it. This did not mean that the author tried very hard to fit the story to the teller in tone and style, to "make them sound as if such and such a character was actually telling them": the histories were supposed to be interesting and exciting stories in their own right, they were there to diversify and to swell the bulk of the romance, not to reflect light on the character of the people who told them. It was not psychological inappropriateness, but actual physical impossibilities, that gave offence to those writers in the seventeenth century who criticized the blatant unlikeliness of the romances, and who often concentrated on the histories. For example, how could a storyteller inside a romance describe a scene where he had not himself been present, or describe thoughts that had never been uttered, or remember every word of the long letters that he was so often given to quoting? It was perceived, often with rather uncalled-for zeal and attention to detail,[18] that all this omniscience was not *vraisemblable*, and satirical remarks on the prodigious feats of memory involved in the verbatim repetition of long letters and conversations became common in romances and prefaces (see below, IV:v). The later romance-writers became defensive. *Astrée* had provided such beauties as letters, which were a very popular *locus* for the demonstration of fine writing, quite confidently and unapologetically; its imitators on the other hand often try to explain how the narrator happened to retain the letters, or to learn them by heart, or how they happened to overhear private conversations: "Je lus cette lettre que j'ay apprise depuis par cœur, au moyen de la coppie que Marsinde m'en donna," "je la puis bien reciter à cause que j'en fis une coppie, et l'ay tant de fois lue, que je me ressouviens fort bien que les termes estoient ceux-cy."[19] There is a certain pathos in these well-meant efforts to avoid impossibilities. Magendie considers the intention far worthier than the result:

... parfois, la maladresse de la justification est singulière. Sélisandre raconte l'amour qu'il a inspiré à la jeune Cariste, pour laquelle il n'éprouve que de l'aversion; elle lui adresse une lettre; "j'y lus, dit-il, ces paroles que j'ay apprises par cœur". Qu'un amant s'attache à graver dans sa mémoire les paroles d'une maîtresse aimée, passe encore! Mais celles d'une femme détestée ... ![20]

These flatfooted beginnings of a dramatic point of view hardly produce superior illusion. They are both over-hopeful and not nearly radical enough. They cannot have blocked unfriendly criticism very effectively, either. To

---

[18] See Magendie, *Le Roman français*, pp. 151 ff.
[19] These examples are quoted by Magendie in *Le Roman français*, pp. 113–14.
[20] Ibid., p. 114.

point out that a letter was for some reason retained by heart, or a conversation overheard by a slave behind an arras, is more likely to direct the reader's attention to the remaining ninety-nine impossibilities than to reconcile him to the patched-up hundredth, which might otherwise have escaped his notice; it will merely put him on his mettle as a critic. Such "realism" could only place heavier stress on the unlikeliness of the whole, just as the reader of *Clarissa* would be much less troubled by the practical difficulties of so much letter-writing if Richardson did not take such noticeable pains to prove that it could very well have been done.

The old and popular method of stringing a collection of tales together by means of a frame story, à la *Decamerone*, allows the voice of the "author" to disappear altogether from the tales which are told by one or more characters in the frame story. The author speaks through fictional narrators in these, usually employing a different one in each story, and his own voice only appears in the frame story. In practice, however, the fictional narrators are as weakly characterized and as illogically omniscient in these collections as in the histories inside the romances. The problem of how the narrator comes by information about states of mind and private conversations applies to these too, of course, and much the same stratagems are used to circumvent it. But the awareness of the problem becomes much more acute in the shorter forms of fiction which oust the long romance in France after 1660.[21]

In the historical novels of Segrais and his followers it is solved in basically the same way as in the clumsy early attempts that I have described, but more thoroughly and successfully. The writer claims to have special means of information—letters, diaries—and very often authenticates the stories, in a way that is psychologically rather than logically convincing, by placing the main characters on the outskirts of "real" history, and allowing the people who are central in history—kings and queens and statesmen—to appear on the outskirts of the novel. Of course this technique was to remain popular for centuries: the principle is the same in Scott's novels.

Some types of historical fiction tangled the problem of illusion and credibility by involving it in the problem of truth, sometimes perhaps in order to try to meet the moral and religious objections to "lies." These forms, "secret histories," "annals," memoirs, sometimes even had some slight basis to their claims to truth, and their popularity gathered momentum throughout the period, reaching a climax in the nineties.[22] It was mainly a French fashion, as far as the production went, but it was consumed even more enthusiastically in England than in France.[23]

---

[21] See Deloffre, *La Nouvelle en France*, passim.
[22] See Adam, *Histoire de la littérature française au XVIIe siècle*, V, 314–17.
[23] Mish, "English Short Fiction," p. 280.

But the distinction between truth and fiction was reasserted by other writers.[24] Challes, in his preface to *Les Illustres Français* (1713), disclaimed historical truth for his work and asserted that he had, on the contrary, sprinkled it with deliberate anachronisms to avoid any confusion on the point.[25] This is interesting, because Challes represents a high point in the development of illusionism, in the art of inducing suspension of disbelief.

Although *Les Illustres Français* is a single whole, a novel, it is also a development of the *Decamerone* or *Canterbury Tales* kind of collection, where tales are told by a group of people to each other. The difference is that in *Les Illustres Français*, after a short introductory scene where two of the principal characters meet, the events are unfolded by a variety of narrators who are at the same time the protagonists of their own and of each other's narratives. I need not describe the dramatic possibilities of such a structure, since it has turned out to play such an important part in the subsequent history of the novel. It is a beginning, capable as later development has shown of infinite variations and sophistications, of what Lubbock calls the dramatized point of view:

> If the story-teller is *in* the story himself, the author is dramatized; his assertions gain in weight, for they are backed by the presence of the narrator in the pictured scene. It is advantage scored; the author has shifted his responsibility, and it now falls where the reader can see and measure it; the arbitrary quality which may at any time be detected in the author's voice is disguised in the voice of his spokesman. Nothing is now imported into the story from without; it is self-contained, it has no associations with anyone beyond its circle.[26]

Lubbock's *Craft of Fiction* is a monument to the conception of fiction as illusion, as the craft of inducing suspension of disbelief in the reader. The technique of *dis*illusion has always flourished by the side of it, however; the author who glories in the "arbitrary quality" of his creation, and is interested in revealing, not disguising it, is as old as the illusionist. The "self-conscious narrator" of Marivaux and Fielding who openly discusses the details of his craft

---

[24] Of course there were many throughout the period who disapproved of pseudo-history and who were careful to point out that their own writings were wholly fictitious; my distinction is not meant to be chronological, or to suggest that one school of thought ousted another. Pierre Bayle criticized the confusion of fiction and truth in the historical novel in his *Dictionnaire historique et critique* (1695—97), in the article on Mme de Villedieu: in his opinion, she had "ouvert la porte à une license dont on abuse tous les jours de plus en plus" (which was indeed the trend in the nineties, as I pointed out above): "C'est celle de prêter ses inventions et ses intrigues galantes aux plus grands hommes des derniers siècles, et de les mêler avec des faits qui ont quelque fondement dans l'histoire. Ce mélange de la vérité et de la fable se répand dans une infinité de livres nouveaux, perd le goût des jeunes gens, et fait que l'on n'ose croire ce qui au fond est croyable" (quoted by Deloffre in *La Nouvelle en France*, p. 57).

[25] See Deloffre, *La Nouvelle en France*, pp. 85 ff.

[26] Percy Lubbock, *The Craft of Fiction* (1921; rpt. London, 1954), pp. 251—52.

with the reader is such a disillusionist, and so is the facetious narrator of Congreve. His funniest effects are based on parody, and the developments towards dramatic realism which were taking place in the somewhat forlorn and apparently unpromising way which I have outlined provided him with an excellent foil. The self-conscious narrator wantons in the wake of the developing taste for "self-contained" fiction, already far advanced in *Les Illustres Français*. His jokes are conservative, not radical: they parody, not the old-established rampaging inconsistencies, but the new and often unfortunate attempts to be consistent, the new awareness of the advantages of a realistic limitation of the knowledge of the narrator. The quotations from *Incognita* which I collected above (III:i) in order to show the acrobatic versatility with which the narrator changes his stance as required exemplify the kind of play that can be made with such an awareness. With regard to the point of view and general attitude of the narrator, Congreve is not merely uninterested in consistency; he has collected in his small compass an absolute encyclopedia of current and popular angles and given it a good stir. This is a typical way of phrasing a change of scene:

... several ladies of her acquaintance came to accompany her to the place designed for the Tilting, where we will leave them drinking Chocolate till 'tis time for them to go. (p. 62)

Well, we will leave them both fretting and contriving to no purpose, to look about and see what was done at the Palace, where their doom was determined much quicker than they imagined. (p. 66)

This kind of transition, "leaving" a set of characters safely occupied and turning to another set, which shows the narrator as conscientiously anxious to tell the reader everything (he leaves no gaps where characters might conceivably get up to their own devices, but is careful to indicate what happens "in the meantime"), is common in the French romances earlier in the century: "On le porte dans un chambre où nous le laisserons pour aller trouver Julliane," "Mais laissons Antiochus guerir à son aise, et retournons où nous avons laissé Araxes."[27] The image is that of the narrator flitting bodily from scene to scene and reporting what he sees; an image which it is difficult to hold simultaneously with that of him compiling his account from various learned and/or old documents, or from hearsay:

'Tis strange now, but all Accounts agree, that just here Leonora, who had run like a violent Stream against Aurelian hitherto, now retorted with as much precipitation in his Favour. I could never get any Body to give me a satisfactory reason, for her suddain and dextrous Change of Opinion just at that stop, which made me conclude she could not help it; ... (pp. 60–61)

[27] Quoted by Magendie (p. 454), who suggests that the formula ("assez gauche") derives from Ariosto.

Such sudden calling-up of nameless authorities is one of the most popular tricks of seventeenth-century comic writing. "Some," explains the author of *The Cimmerian Matron* at the mention of a mantle which plays some part in the plot, "will have it to be only a blanket."[28] Who will? A ghostly dispute about blankets and mantles is apparently taking place among the authorities on the subject. Butler judiciously refuses to take sides over another weighty crux:

> But here our Authors make a doubt,
> Whether he were more wise, or stout.
> Some hold the one, and some the other.[29]
> (*Hudibras*, I, 1, 29—31)

As for the serious usage which gives savour to the joke, I presume that in the case of Butler it does not come from fiction. Rather, the "soul" of his quip is the reverential pedantry with which minor details in the classical epics were disagreed upon by the learned. The lines from *Hudibras* are an early manifestation of the spirit in which Swift and Pope were to attack Bentley and Theobald.[30]

There is, too, something of Swift's comic orgies of scientific quasi-learning in Congreve's unexpected conjuring up of "Chymists" to give a pedantic explanation of a perfectly commonplace circumstance (the fact that the torches dispel the dark):

> ...for Madam Night was no more to be seen than she was to be heard; and the Chymists were of Opinion, That her fuliginous Damps, rarefy'd by the abundance of Flame, were evaporated. (p. 39)

The Royal Society "pedants" were popular butts for the wits. But usually Congreve has a more literary "soul" for his mock-ignorance and more or less uncalled-for speculations about reasons and explanations. Pedantry is no adequate soul for the "blanket" aside fom *The Cimmerian Matron*, with its sudden blurred glimpse of learned sources being researched by the author, or for the slightly different ignorance affected by Congreve in *Incognita*:

> ...which Aurelian understanding, groped for the Knots, and either untied them or cut them asunder; but 'tis more probable the latter, because more expeditious. (p. 72)

---

[28] Charles C. Mish, ed., *Restoration Prose Fiction* (Lincoln, 1970), p. 153; cf. Mish's introduction to *The Cimmerian Matron* in this anthology, p. 146.

[29] Sturgis E. Leavitt ("Paul Scarron and English Travesty," *SP*, 16, 1919, 108—20) traces the "humoristic touch of citing vague authority for unimportant detail" to Scarron's *Virgile travesti*.

[30] See A. C. Guthkelch and D. Nichol Smith, ed., *"A Tale of a Tub": To which is added "The Battle of the Books" and "The Mechanical Operation of the Spirit"* (1920; 2nd ed. Oxford, 1958), pp. xlvii—li and 211—58; and James Sutherland, ed., *The Dunciad*, The Twickenham Edition of the Poems of Alexander Pope, V (London, 1943), passim.

There is no hinting at authorities here, but instead an educated guess as to what is most likely to have happened; however, the detail is fully as unimportant as anything in *Hudibras* or *The Cimmerian Matron*. The soul, the serious practice which gives relish to the mocking use, I take to be in this case the realistic or would-be realistic "artificial limitation of a narrator who in other respects shows himself to be omniscient,"[31] as used by Aphra Behn in the passage which I quoted above (p. 24). Her skilful use of a realistic limitation of source material, eked out with helpful guesswork, creates a more immediate and convincing picture for the reader: the same technique which Lubbock admires and analyses in much later writers. Nevertheless, one can at the same time see why the device would invite parody, and why Congreve should treat the reader to *his* helpful piece of logic with regard to Aurelian's technique for loosening ropes.

Apra Behn's admission of ignorance is a sophisticated way of gaining conviction and credibility. The older literature, which I have exemplified by the dominant romance, preferred to explain how the narrator happened to know everything, as we have seen above. Congreve does this too. His favourite source, when for some reason he pretends to need one, is Aurelian. Of course he knows everything without explanations and sources when he wants to, and there is always a particular reason for introducing the testimony of Aurelian, besides the general reason of imitating and parodying the would-be realistic sources in the romances, such as the eavesdropping slave. Thus, for example, the impassioned description of Incognita at the ball (p. 52), an antithetic setpiece of alluring yet commanding looks and piercing eyes, turns out at the end to be the product of the young lover's own passion and rhetoric. Immediately after the piece of "fine writing" which I quote in full in section IV:iv below, Congreve writes:

> But Aurelian (from whom I had every tittle of her Description) fancy'd he saw a little Nest of Cupids break from the Tresses of her Hair, and every one officiously betake himself to his task.

The too-rhetorical description which has gone before is now justified: the parenthesis makes it into a sardonic comment on Aurelian's infatuation and resort to conventional hyperbole. The same thing happens later, where Congreve's own brisk and efficient narrative is suspended for a positively *précieuse* style, in the decription of Incognita's becoming mournfulness and Aurelian's display of sensibility:

> At that (as Aurelian tells the story) a Sigh diffused a mournful sweetness through the Air, and liquid grief fell gently from her Eyes, triumphant sadness sat upon her Brow,

---

[31] Wayne C. Booth, *The Rhetoric of Fiction* (Chicago, 1961), p. 184, n.

and even sorrow seem'd delighted with the Conquest he had made. See what a change Aurelian felt! His Heart bled Tears, and trembled in his Breast; Sighs struggling for a vent had choaked each others passage up: His Floods of Joy were all suppresst; cold doubts and fears had chill'd 'em with a sudden Frost, and he was troubled to excess; yet knew not why. (p. 74)

It is not surprising that Congreve feels the need to counteract these poetic raptures with his own worldly tone:

Well, the Learned say it was Sympathy: and I am always of the Opinion with the Learned, if they speak first.

iii. The Self-Conscious Narrator

Of course the intrusive narrator does not manifest himself in neat incisions of commentary into an otherwise neutrally reported fabric. Philosophically speaking, there is no such thing as a neutral narrative.[32] However, rather than pursue a logical definition of seventeenth-century "facetious" or intrusive or self-conscious storytelling, with the necessarily attendant subdivisons and ramifications, all of which seemed uncalled-for in a study of this kind, I have tried more empirically to indicate where these narratives belong on the scale of conspicuousness of the narrator. The scale may be thought of as ranging from the total absence of the narrator in dramatic dialogue, to his total presence in the first-person novel, where every sentence is a remark made by the narrating "I" to the reader. I have relied, perhaps rather heavily, on the assumption that one knows more or less what is meant by words like "intrusive." On the same principle, I have used "intrusion" loosely, without trying to answer the question of how overt or distracting or even how long an interruption should be to constitute an intrusion. To ask this question seems reasonable in a case where opposed extremes are clearly distinguishable, but the more neutral area where the two shade into each other makes the fixing of any precise boundary between them an arbitrary undertaking. Congreve's pervasive, mildly cynical tone in *Incognita* is self-conscious, in the ordinary sense of that word, all the time.

Wayne C. Booth, however, chooses a specialized and technical definition of "self-consciousness" in his article "The Self-Conscious Narrator in Comic Fiction Before *Tristram Shandy*," in order to deal with one particular aspect of this comic fiction. Booth examines, not mere "moralizing interruptions," but

---

[32] Cf. Wayne C. Booth: "In *all* written works there is an implied narrator or 'author' who 'intrudes' in making the necessary choices to get his story or his argument or his exposition written in the way he desires" ("The Self-Conscious Narrator in Comic Fiction Before *Tristram Shandy*," PMLA, 67, 1952, 164).

only "the self-conscious narrator who intrudes into his novel to comment on himself as a writer, and on his book, not simply as a series of events with moral implications, but as a created literary product."[33] This kind of comment is frequently made by Congreve in *Incognita*, and these "digressions" as he himself calls them are often singled out when critics try to define the special flavour of the book.

The ostensible purpose of Congreve's digressions is usually to put the reader in his place, in a comic reversal of the flattery of the reader and the appeals to his candour and judiciousness which appear so often in the prefaces of his contemporaries. Congreve—or "Congreve," the narrator—shows no such deference.

On the evening of the great ball, Congreve amplifies the phenomenon of torchlight with a faded Elizabethan fertility of metaphor. The "*æquilibrium*" of day and night, which ordinarily at that time of the evening "holds the Air in a gloomy suspence between an unwillingness to leave the light, and a natural impulse into the Dominion of darkness," is disturbed by the prodigious number of torches, so that

the day, by help of these Auxiliary Forces, seem'd to continue its Dominion; the Owls and Bats apprehending their mistake, in counting the hours, retir'd again to a convenient darkness; for Madam Night was no more to be seen than she was to be heard; and the Chymists were of Opinion, That her fuliginous Damps, rarefy'd by the abundance of Flame, were evaporated. (p. 39)

By 1692 this is a distinctly old-fashioned kind of rhetoric, spreading out from the slightest of occasions, with its beautiful long words and pseudo-scientific explanations (cf. p. 34 above). It is mildly annoying to a reader who wants to get on with the story, but it does not actually take very long, so Congreve takes it as an opportunity to be playfully impolite to the reader in a rather longer mock apology:

Now the Reader I suppose to be upon Thorns at this and the like impertinent Digressions, but let him alone and he'll come to himself; at which time I think fit to acquaint him, that when I digress, I am at that time writing to please my self, when I continue the Thread of the Story, I write to please him; supposing him a reasonable Man, I conclude him satisfied to allow me this liberty, and so I proceed.

This is the first of his "self-conscious" digressions, in Booth's sense, and it establishes control very effectively with its superior tone ("think fit to acquaint him") and its not very hidden suggestion that the reader is too lowbrow to appreciate anything beyond "the Thread of the Story": a suggestion which, as we have seen (see Introduction above), was taken only too literally by the

---

[33] Ibid., p. 165.

ingenious Corinna. This supposed obtuseness in the reader makes it necessary to appeal to an absurd principle of fair division between his taste and that of the author; that the acceptance of such a principle would prove the reader "a reasonable Man," which Congreve politely assumes that he is, is an ironic reversal of the usual appeals to the "candid reader."

Later on, he again assumes a certain position on the part of the reader, in order to point out what a stupid position it is. Leonora has mistaken the masked Hippolito for her cousin Lorenzo, and when Hippolito writes to apologize for conniving at the deception, she soon reasons herself into a liking of the deceiver. His letter is so well written, after all, and she also recalls "something of a more becoming Air in the Stranger than was usual to Lorenzo" (p. 60). Also, she believes him to be Aurelian (he is using Aurelian's name, for complicated but honourable reasons), and she knows the "quality" of Aurelian by repute.

> I would not have the Reader now be impertinent, and look upon this to be force, or a whim of the Author's, that a Woman should proceed so far in her Approbation of a Man whom she never saw, that it is impossible, therefore ridiculous to suppose it. Let me tell such a Critick, that he knows nothing of the Sex, if he does not know that a Woman may be taken with the Character and Description of a Man, when general and extraordinary, that she may be prepossess'd with an agreeable Idea of his Person and Conversation; and though she cannot imagine his real Features, or manner of Wit, yet she has a general Notion of what is call'd a fine Gentleman, and is prepar'd to like such a one who does not disagree with that Character. (p. 61)

After a few general observations on the uses and dangers of imagination in such cases, Congreve goes on:

> I could find it in my Heart to beg the Reader's pardon for this Digression, if I thought he would be sensible of the Civility; for I promise him, I do not intend to do it again throughout the Story, though I make never so many, and though he take them never so ill. But because I began this upon a bare Supposition of his Impertinence, which might be somewhat impertinent in me to suppose, I do, and hope to make him amends by telling him, that by the time Leonora was dress'd, several Ladies of her acquaintance ... (p. 62)

And so the story is re-launched.

Logically, Congreve has started with a discussion of the psychological probability of Leonora's reaction—that is, of his "series of events with moral implications"—and rounded it off by moving on to the plane of the "created literary product" in the second passage, where he explains why he apologizes for the digression, and what he intends to do about future digressions. But it is characteristic of *Incognita* that this distinction seems pointless. The two passages are tied together by their playful abuse of the reader: first it is assumed that he is on the point of being "impertinent" in his critical objections; then, more infernally, it is supposed to be scarcely worth while to apologize to him, since he is unlikely to be "sensible of the Civility." Moreover, even while discussing the question of probability, Congreve is actually explicitly defending Leonora as a "created literary product":

> ... that it is impossible, therefore ridiculous to suppose it.

Leonora's reaction is something he chooses to "suppose," to invent, not something he has merely to report; just as he sometimes chooses to apologize for a digression. The invention is of course defended by an appeal to experience: it is not impossible, therefore not ridiculous as an invention. The reasonable and "realistic," if rather over-earnest, analysis of the psychological mechanism behind reactions such as Leonora's is twisted abruptly in the last sentence into a pleasantly deadpan satirical observation which seems to put Leonora unexpectedly on the same level as the marriage-obsessed young girls of Restoration comedy who are prepared to like any "man of fashion" (like Hippolita in Wycherley's *Gentleman Dancing-Master*, 1672):

> ... yet she has a general Notion of what is call'd a fine Gentleman, and is prepar'd to like such a one who does not disagree with that Character.

This quip is amusing because it is put so quietly; but really the satirical sentiment is so literary, so well-worn in the comedies, that the strong literary association undercuts the appeal to reality, to the possible. The impression of artificiality is not produced because Congreve is careless or inept at creating a sense of reality; but rather because he is careful not to. What really happens in the quoted passages is that the reader is manœuvred into accepting, for the fun of it, the position of being talked down to, knowing that Congreve the real narrator knows that "Congreve" the persona-narrator of the moment is unjustified in his assumptions. Congreve and the reader share a joke at the expense of the charmingly eccentric "Congreve," the persona-narrator, and at this "Congreve's" unwitting parody of contemporary fiction.

Apparently, the self-conscious meta-digression where the author stands back and looks at his book as a book, as something he is inventing, is so integrated in the texture of *Incognita* that there is little point in singling it out as Booth does. Moreover, it is not as avant-garde as Booth suggests; it seems as if Booth, writing in 1951, underestimated the popularity of the "facetious" style in England. The device of self-consciousness, he writes,

> had been used successfully by Cervantes, Scarron, Furetière, and Congreve for comic ornament and for incidental parody of more serious writers. But their relatively skilful usage had little effect on comic writers generally. In England the "facetious" style was perhaps considered best fit for foreigners; at any rate, Congreve's lead—perhaps because his novel was never widely read—was not followed by English novelists.[34]

---

[34] Ibid., p. 170.

As I tried to show above, the mocking, amusedly detached way of telling the story in *Incognita* was in fact the height of fashion at the time of its publication, although Congreve used the manner with much more wit and grace than was common. The same applies to the special kind of self-consciousness that Booth is interested in: Charles C. Mish, using the word in the same sense, writes that "the self-conscious narrator is in full bloom" in the novelettes in the *Gentleman's Journal* of Peter Motteux (1692—94), and cites some striking instances. Consequently Congreve's originality in this respect is not that of the pioneer; nevertheless he digresses in a more elaborate, and more elaborately and complexly ironical way, than his contemporaries.

iv. The Conciseness of Congreve

Congreve's *Incognita*, then, was published at the height of a fashion which was at the time loosely labelled "the manner of Scarron," and which obviously influenced it very much. However, Congreve's delicate handling of the fashionable pattern makes his style very different from the ordinary English conception of the Scarronian manner. Mish considers the novels of Scarron, together with those of Aphra Behn, as the main influence on *Incognita*,[35] and it may well have been directly influenced by the master as well as by the current English scene: Congreve owned the French 1665 edition of Scarron's novels at his death in 1729.[36] In any case, *Incognita* is more like Scarron's novels, in delicacy as well as in elaborate "self-consciousness," than it is like the much cruder anglicized version of the manner. The facetious vogue in England is heavily explicit. A humorous point is, in general, underscored and spelled out at length, to make sure that the meanest intelligence will get it; this is especially so in the debased Grub Street facetiousness of Tom Brown and Peter Motteux. It also leans towards a pointless "vivacious" chattiness, with a lot of "well's" and "why's." Congreve is capable of using this latter feature for reasons of his own, as in the passage on p. 51: "Well, what follow'd? Well,[37] she pull'd off her Mask, and appear'd to him at once in the Glory of Beauty." This comes in consequence of Aurelian's being offered the choice of knowing Incognita's real name or seeing her face and rapturously embracing the second alternative, and it serves to point the anticlimax: a girl removing the mask from her face. The whole passage is very finely balanced between the visionary and the down-to-

---

[35] "English Short Fiction," p. 299, n. 121.
[36] See John C. Hodges, *The Library of William Congreve* (New York, 1955), p. 97, No. 571. Congreve was certainly acquainted with the English translation as well: Bellmour in *The Old Batchelour*, who disguises himself as a priest in order to debauch a married lady, is appropriately armed with a copy of "trusty *Scarron*'s Novels" in place of a prayer-book (IV.ii).
[37] "Why" in the first edition.

earth. It is only superficially that Congreve is being chatty here: in fact he is being extremely economical.

The pervasive impression of Congreve's style is that of restraint: understatement instead of elaboration. His sardonic attitude towards the over-predictable responses of his young heroes is indicated with the most urbane lightness:

Having her still by the Hand, which he squeez'd somewhat more eagerly than is usual for Cousins to do, ... (p. 46)

There arose another Sigh; a Sympathy seiz'd Aurelian immediately: (For by the Way, sighing is as catching among Lovers, as yawning among the Vulgar.) Beside hearing the Name of Love, made him fetch such a Sigh, that Hippolito's were but Fly-blows in Comparison, that was answered with all the Might Hippolito had, Aurelian ply'd him close till they were both out of Breath. (pp. 55—56)

This sighing contest has amused several critics.[38] As far as the French romances were concerned, the remark on the contagiousness of sighing among lovers is no more than just: Dorothy Dallas writes that "la maladie des soupirs," which is an important characteristic of the perfect lover, "est non seulement chronique: elle devient contagieuse."[39]

The same urbanity is displayed in the bland little parenthesis of the next quotation, which describes the practical difficulties which stand in the way of the heroes' newly conceived affections. Aurelian repents, for his part, that he was so improvident as to choose rather to see Incognita's face than to know her name, when he had the chance, while

Hippolito on the other side (though Aurelian thought him in a much better Way) was no less afflicted for himself. (p. 57)

In this passage, the irony is nicely distributed between our heroes:

Aurelian laid himself down to rest, that is, upon the Bed; for he was a better Lover than to pretend to sleep that Night, while Hippolito set himself again to frame his Letter design'd for Leonora. He writ several, at last pitched upon one, and very probably the worst, as you may guess when you read it in its proper Place. (p. 58)

Congreve's particular show-piece, the brilliantly artificial conversation between Incognita and Aurelian at the ball, is a cascade of epigrams where the only restraining influence is the polite proviso that the lady must remain one up. Aurelian is most of the time something of a stooge for the wit of Incognita, although he is once allowed to turn her own words to his advantage in a way which shows great presence of mind. This is where Incognita, in reproof of his

---

[38] Cf. Sir Walter Raleigh, *The English Novel* (London, 1896), p. 102; and H. F. B. Brett-Smith, ed., *Incognita*, The Percy Reprints, No. 5 (Oxford, 1922), pp. x, xii.

[39] Dorothy Dallas, *Le Roman français de 1660 à 1680* (Paris, 1932), pp. 37—38; the description is substantiated by ample quotation.

ravings about dying of love for her, assures him that his sudden passion is "too violent to be lasting."

> He replied, Indeed it might not be very lasting, (with a submissive mournful Voice) but it would continue during his Life.[40] (p. 53)

The wit of the word-fencers, fairly represented by this sample, is often pleasantly concise, but not exactly underplayed and understated in the way which gives such a special tone to the voice of Congreve's narrator. A beautiful exception, however, is that brisk reply by Incognita which Aurelian very understandably does not "know well what to make of":

> He only told her he was too mean a Conquest for her wit who was already a Slave to the Charms of her Person. She thanked him for his Complement, and briskly told him she ought to have made him a return in praise of his wit, but she hoped he was a Man more happy than to be dissatisfy'd with any of his own Endowments; and if it were so, that he had not a just Opinion of himself, she knew her self incapable of saying any thing to beget one. (p. 43)

That the characteristic conciseness of Congreve's narrative should coexist very successfully with "the intrusive narrator" is not a paradox. The intrusions and digressions do not elaborate or explain points already made, they are *new* points. This being so, it is only logical that we even find concise and underplayed intrusions, like the second sentence in this description of the beauty of Incognita:

> In short, to be made sensible of his condition, we must conceive some Idea of what he beheld, which is not to be imagined till seen, nor then to be express'd. Now see the impertinence and conceitedness of an Author, who will have a fling at a Description, which he has Prefaced with an impossiblity. One might have seen something in her Composition resembling the Formation of Epicurus his World, as if every Atome of Beauty had concurr'd to unite an excellency. (p. 51)

He goes on to describe her, in what amounts to a purple patch of rays and flames and antitheses:

> Such Majesty and Affability were in her Looks; so alluring, yet commanding was her Presence, that it mingled awe with love; kindling a Flame which trembled to aspire.

The aside about impertinence and conceitedness alerts the reader for a conscious enjoyment of the rhetoric that follows, and which turns out in the end, as I pointed out above, to be a product of the poetic vein of Aurelian himself. Of course the "soul" of Congreve's joke here is that to "have a fling at a

---

[40] Apparently it is possible to miss the point of this reference to the probable shortness of his life (because he will soon die of love), since Günter Schopper does (*Aufbau und Sprache von Congreves "Incognita,"* Diss. Mainz 1967, pp. 88—89), while still finding it a witty example of *conciliatio* and *correctio*; cf. III:v below.

Description, which he has Prefaced with an impossibility" is such an old and enduringly popular trick ("negatio") for adding a rather meaningless kind of elegance to a description.

The conciseness of Congreve implies great confidence in the sensitivity and alertness of the reader. His poise in *Incognita* is nearly always perfect. It must be admitted, however, that he occasionally does go on, after a beautifully restrained joke, and spoil it with a heavyhandedness which deserves that name only by his own standards. For example, the sardonic tone in which Congreve describes how Hippolito hides behind a myrtle bush, shaded by a bay tree, to wait unseen for his mistress, is extremely good; its avoidance of open jocularity is worthy of *The Way of the World*:

> He was delighted with the Choice he had made, for he found a Hollow in the Myrtle, as if purposely contriv'd for the Reception of one Person, who might undiscovered perceive all about him. He looked upon it as a good Omen, that the Tree Consecrated to Venus was so propitious to him in his Amorous Distress. The Consideration of that, together with the Obligation he lay under to the Muses, for sheltering him also with so large a Crown of Bays, had like to have set him a Rhyming. (p. 78)

In the next sentence the smile becomes appreciably broader, however, which is a pity:

> He was, to tell the Truth, naturally addicted to Madrigal, and we should undoubtedly have had a small desert of Numbers to have pick'd and Criticiz'd upon, had he not been interrupted just upon his Delivery; nay, after the Preliminary Sigh had made Way for his Utterance.

But such unnecessary expansion is exceptional. Often Congreve is concise in exactly the way which Bergson considers particularly English:

> Exprimer honnêtement une idée malhonnête, prendre une situation scabreuse, ou un métier bas, ou une conduite vile, et les décrire en termes de stricte *respectability*, cela est généralement comique. J'emploi à dessein un mot anglais: la chose elle-même, en effet, est bien anglaise [...]. Un mot suffira parfois, pourvu que ce mot nous laisse entrevoir tout un système de transposition accepté dans un certain milieu, et qu'il nous révèle, en quelque sorte, une organisation morale de l'immoralité. Je ne citerai ici que cette observation d'un haut fonctionnaire à un de ses subordonnés, dans un roman de Gogol: "Tu voles trop pour un fonctionnaire de ton grade."[41]

This is just the kind of transposition Congreve makes when he writes that the revenge which Don Fabritio had sworn to take on Cousin Lorenzo was to devolve, in case Lorenzo died before it could be executed on him, "upon his next of Kin, and so to descend Lineally like an English Estate, to all the Heirs Males of this Family" (p. 49).[42] In general, to suggest a transposition of a detail

---

[41] Henri Bergson, *Le Rire* (1900; rpt. Paris, 1913), pp. 128–29.
[42] Cf. H. F. B. Brett-Smith, ed., *Incognita*, p. xiii.

into a system where it does not belong—which is too large, or too solemn, or otherwise incongruous—is perhaps the most economical form of wit of all. In the sighing scene which I quoted above (p. 41), Congreve implies such a system in his aside that "sighing is as catching among Lovers, as yawning among the Vulgar." The opposition "Lovers"—"the Vulgar" suggests that lovers are a sort of chosen people, forming the highest level in a whole dimly glimpsed social hierarchy: in other words, the whole mock-universe of the *précieuse* art of love is conjured up for a brief instant.

A still briefer and more concentrated glimpse of the same universe is offered by Hippolito, in his precocious reflexion on the risks of revealing himself as a stranger to Leonora, who believes that the man who is taking her home through the darkened streets is Cousin Lorenzo:

> He knew Women were apt to shriek or swoon upon such Occasions, and should she happen to do either, he might be at a loss how to bring himself off. (p. 47)

The conception which is revealed here of a whole well-known class of "such Occasions," with stereotyped proper responses from the lady, can only come from the romances and comedies of the seventeenth century, with their profusion of masks, mixed-up identities and unmaskings.

v. "Rhetoric"

Günter Schopper has in his dissertation *Aufbau und Sprache von Congreves "Incognita"* a lengthy analysis of Congreve's use of rhetoric,[43] but the limits of his discussion are nevertheless excessively narrow. By rhetoric he understands school rhetoric (p. 71), and his terms and subdivisions are taken not from any Restoration authority or handbook, but from H. Lausberg, *Elemente der literarischen Rhetorik* (2nd ed., München, 1963). By classifying according to Lausberg, firstly, the syntactical variations from ordinary statement—rhetorical questions, anacoluthia, ellipses, etc.—in the dialogue of *Incognita*, and secondly the use in it of rhetorical figures such as parallelisms and oxymora, he concludes that Congreve "genau [. . .] diesen Vorschriften folgt" (p. 86). In so far as this is true it is a truism. Schopper's first category, rhetorical questions and so on, are the commonplaces of the facetious style, and Congreve uses them rather less than the other comic writers. His second category, the figures, are of course the commonplaces of Restoration literature in general; again, if Congreve's use of rhetoric in this sense is remarkable at all, it is for its spareness. Restoration fiction (not to mention plays and poetry) swims in a sea of oxymora. Antithesis as ornament, as delightful in and for itself,

---

[43] Diss. Mainz 1967, pp. 71–100.

might be discredited for the purposes of discursive writing by the new fashion for "plain style,"[44] but it remained the cornerstone of the second-rate "elegant." Moreover, it was the chief ornament of *précieuse* conversation: gallantry was not gallantry without antithesis, parallelism and chiasmus. By 1692, such preciousness of utterance was ridiculous to the fastidious: the watered-down Euphuism of the amorous dialogue in *Incognita* is Congreve showing off, certainly; but it is also Congreve making fun of the over-ambitiousness of his heroes in the field of compliments. He does not condescend to use such fireworks except in the dialogue, or in a special "self-conscious" way. As we have seen above (III:iii), when he does describe the grief of Incognita, and the sympathetic grief of Aurelian, in a burst of laboured antitheses, this way of going on is explicitly attributed to Aurelian's way of telling the story, and is accompanied by a deflating rider by the narrator. Aurelian appears here as almost a devotee of Le Pays; but Congreve himself was not.

This is not to say that his language is exactly colloquial, either. Concise, elegant and selective, it is the opposite of the realistic style which Ian Watt describes, which is authenticated by verboseness and repetition and "works by exhaustive presentation rather than elegant concentration."[45] The guiding principle of Congreve's language is always wit. But it is not the wit of symmetry and antithesis. Compared to the language of Sidney's *Arcadia*, the language of *Incognita* is indeed colloquial: supple, flexible, natural. This is a very obvious observation, but it seems to me worth making, because in another important respect *Arcadia* and *Incognita* are much alike. Their plots are alike. The plot of *Incognita* exhibits the same intricate symmetry as that of *Arcadia*; but in *Arcadia*, this plot is expressed in congenial language. In *Incognita* it is expressed in the idiom of "the manner of Scarron."

The congruence between plot and style in *Arcadia* is analysed by E. M. Waith in *The Pattern of Tragicomedy in Beaumont and Fletcher*.[46] W. W. Greg had condemned the rhetoric of "Arcadianism," as

> little if at all better than Euphuism. It is just as formal, just as much a trick, just as stilted and unpliable, just as painful an illustration of the fact that a figure of rhetoric may be an occasional ornament, but cannot by any degree of ingenuity be made to serve as a basis of composition.

To this Waith replies that Sidney's rhetoric does precisely "serve as a basis of composition." As a typical example of Arcadianism, he quotes the lament of Zelmane (Pyrocles disguised) for the difficult situation of being beloved by

---

[44] See J. E. Spingarn, ed., *Critical Essays of the Seventeenth Century*, I (Oxford, 1908), xxxvi–xlviii.

[45] Ian Watt, *The Rise of the Novel* (1957; rpt. London: Pelican Books, 1971), p. 33.

[46] Yale Studies in English, No. 120 (New Haven, 1952), pp. 75–76.

both king Basilius and queen Gynecia while himself in love with their daughter Philoclea:

> But *Zelmane* being ridde of this loving, but little-loved company, Alas (said she) poore *Pyrocles*, was there ever one, but I, that had received wrong, and could blame no body? that having more then I desire, am still in want of that I woulde? Truly Love, I must needes say thus much on thy behalfe; thou hast imployed my love there, where all love is deserved; and for recompence hast sent me more love then ever I desired. But what wilt thou doo *Pyrocles*? which way canst thou finde to ridde thee of thy intricate troubles? To her whom I would be knowne to, I live in darkenesse: and to her am revealed, from whom I would be most secreat. What shift shall I finde against the diligent love of Basilius? what shield against the violent passions of *Gynecia*? And if that be done, yet how am I the neerer to quench the fire that consumes me? Wel, well, sweete *Philoclea*, my whole confidence must be builded in thy divine spirit, which cannot be ignorant of the cruell wound I have received by you.

Waith continues:

> Without a doubt, this is formal, tricky, stilted, and unpliable writing, just as Greg says it is, but the situation it expresses is also formal, tricky, stilted, and unpliable. It is useless to single out the style for disapproval, since it is an inseparable part of the literary form.

Exactly; whereas in *Incognita* a formal, tricky, stilted and unpliable plot is manifested in flexible and straightforward writing. The situations in *Incognita* are just as stylized and intricate as in *Arcadia*: the *plot* is full of the parallelism and antithesis which is absent from the style. It is an "Italian" rather than a "Spanish" plot, to use the terminology of Deloffre (see II:i above): an intricate and tidy pattern of hair-breadth coincidences, lucky mistakes and unlucky ingenuities, peopled by cardboard characters and located in a cardboard Florence.[47] The worldly, knowing manner of telling the story—a manner which is very much of the 1690's and which must have seemed highly contemporary to Congreve's first readers—does not make the matter told seem less artificial and remote, or more "real." The style of Scarron is sometimes called realistic because it is anti-romantic;[48] in Congreve, the manner of Scarron is certainly not an instrument of realism, but serves rather to enhance the artificiality of the "world" of *Incognita*. Charles Muscatine's remark on the difference between Guillaume de Lorris and Guillaume de Machaut can be applied to Sidney and Congreve: "The earlier poet creates in us an astonished belief; the later, with his wink and his knowledge, his little *aperçus*, creates knowing make-believe."[49]

---

[47] The setting is sketchily indicated, although skilfully and with "evident regard for accuracy of detail," demonstrated by E. S. de Beer in "Congreve's *Incognita*: The Source of its Setting, with a Note on Wilson's *Belphegor*," *RES*, 8 (1932), 74—77.

[48] Scarron's editor Henri Bénac objects strongly to this: see his introduction to *Œuvres complètes de Scarron* (Paris, 1951), passim.

[49] *Chaucer and the French Tradition*, p. 100.

IV. Structure

i. The Plot

The sophisticated levity of Congreve's presentation of his story naturally makes the reader hope for a corresponding sophistication in that which is presented. Most critics have been disappointed in this hope. In his brief description of *Incognita* in "English Short Fiction," Charles C. Mish voices with admirable clarity an attitude which is implied by many others:

> Written with considerable detachment, with frequent intrusion of the narrative voice, and with much irony, the style has a much more sophisticated and "modern" sound altogether than the content would seem to demand. Hence the label attached to the book will depend largely on whether matter or manner makes the stronger impression. (p. 299)

On the other hand, at least one critic has found the "matter" of *Incognita* extremely symbolic and profound,[1] in a way that would make Congreve's ironic style seem still more inappropriate. I hope to show that the irony of the structure of *Incognita* in fact suits the irony of the style excellently. In order to do this, it is unfortunately necessary to summarize its plot. It is no wonder that critics prefer to concentrate on those aspects of *Incognita* which may be discussed without describing what actually happens in it, for the plot is both too complicated and too airily absurd to be summarized with either grace or brevity. This is the story:

Aurelian, a young man of quality who has been educated in Siena, travels from Siena to Florence where his father lives. He is accompanied by his dear friend Hippolito, a Spaniard. When they arrive in Florence, they find that "Extraordinary Preparations" have been made to solemnize the nuptials of a kinswoman of the great Duke. The festivities, which include a tilting, are to last for three days, and in order to enjoy them to the full Aurelian decides not to join his father immediately. The whole of the succeeding adventure takes place in Florence and within the compass of this celebration, thus satisfying the dramatic "unities" of time and place, as Congreve points out in his

---

[1] Aubrey Williams, "Congreve's *Incognita* and the Contrivances of Providence," *Imagined Worlds: Essays on Some English Novels and Novelists in Honour of John Butt*, ed. Maynard Mack and Ian Gregor (London, 1968), pp. 3–17; cf. IV:iii below.

Preface. The first of the divertissements is a masked ball at court, and here Aurelian falls in love with a witty and beautiful lady who refuses to tell him her name. This is Incognita. Aurelian on his side is afraid that the rumour of his arrival may reach and offend his father, and has the inspiration of telling her that his name is Don Hippolito di Savolina. Meanwhile the real Hippolito, in another part of the room, is accosted by another beautiful lady, Leonora, who mistakes him for her cousin Lorenzo: he is of course masked and has hired a "habit" belonging to this Lorenzo, who lies at home wounded after a duel. In order to scrape an acquaintance Hippolito pretends to be Cousin Lorenzo who has made a surprising recovery, and escorts her home.

Back at their lodgings the young men confer, each thinking his own situation the more hopeless, and decide that since Hippolito's identity is already taken, as it were, he had better call himself Aurelian in his future dealings with Leonora. (This stroke seems less brilliant the more one meditates upon it.) The next day they take part in the tilting, and do very well. The ladies look on and admire, recognizing their admirers by means too complicated to be described here. Unfortunately, Aurelian's father is among the spectators too; he recognizes his son and starts looking for his lodgings. Worse, he speeds up the negotiations for the marriage of Aurelian to a certain accomplished Juliana; an arrangement which is intended to make up an estrangement between the two families involved. At the instigation of the Duke, the fathers set the marriage for the next day, as a fitting climax to the three days' festivities.

When Aurelian hears that he is discovered (for it is "diffused like air" and reaches his lodgings in half an hour) he is torn rather briefly between love and duty. Love wins. After an indescribable mix-up with everybody passing into or out of houses at the exact moment when somebody else is passing out of or into them, so that Aurelian keeps narrowly evading his father and missing his Incognita, he at last finds her, by the luckiest accident in the world, dressed in boy's clothes and on the point of being raped by a ruffian. She too is on the run from an imposed marriage, she says, and he persuades her to promise to marry him.

Leonora has never seen Hippolito's face, but has fallen in love with his becoming air and successful tilting. Since she thinks his name is Aurelian—he has written her a letter to that effect—she is thrown into despair by the rumour of "his" projected marriage to Juliana, and soliloquizes mournfully in her father's garden in an "undress" which adds to "the abundance of her Charms" (compare the boy's clothes of Incognita). By the most fortunate circumstance imaginable, Hippolito overhears her confession of love for him, and they get married in a convent which happens to adjoin the garden, Hippolito arguing that this is the only way to thwart "his father's" plans.

On the last page and last day of the diversions all the characters meet, by a surprising coincidence, in the lodgings of the heroes. Aurelian begs his father's forgiveness and, after some delay and parental huffing, presents his bride who turns out, by a happy chance, to be none other than Juliana herself.

The neatness and tightness of this nonsensical story make a summary unusually difficult: nothing much can be left out because it all hangs together. Congreve describes the effect he has aimed at in his well-known Preface, written to "prevent thy overlooking some little pains which I have taken in the Composition of the following Story" (p. 32). He has imitated dramatic writing, he states, in the "Design, Contexture and Result of the Plot," and is proud of the idea: "I have not observed it before in a Novel":

The design of the Novel is obvious, after the first meeting of Aurelian and Hippolito with Incognita and Leonora, and the difficulty is in bringing it to pass, maugre all apparent obstacles, within the compass of two days. How many probable Casualties intervene in opposition to the main Design, *viz.* of marrying two Couple so oddly engaged in an intricate Amour, I leave the Reader at his leisure to consider: As also whether every Obstacle does not in the progress of the Story act as subservient to that purpose, which at first it seems to oppose. In a Comedy this would be called the Unity of Action; here it may pretend to no more than an Unity of Contrivance. (pp. 33—34)

One admits that the design is obvious, but it is equally transparent that the difficulty is not so much "in bringing [the marriages] to pass, maugre all apparent obstacles, within the compass of two days," but rather in preventing the "obstacles" from being cleared away within the compass of two minutes. In fact there are no real obstacles, because there are no conflicting interests anywhere: there is only misunderstanding. To the nominal character of "the conflict between love and duty" I will return in another context (V:iii below); but I am afraid that my summary does not do justice to the lack of *any* real motivation behind the problems of the heroes. The story exhibits a combination of the silliest sides of Restoration comedy with a happy lack of the ballast of genuine social and economic questions which counteracts the unreality of these plays. However unlikely in details, the later Restoration comedy characteristically centres round some tangible conflict of interests, such as that between the gallant and the city husband, or between the various characters who are or wish to become involved with an heiress. The earlier comedies such as Dryden's sometimes feature the same insouciance with regard to economic motives as *Incognita*, but they treat extra-marital sex as a sort of currency instead; whereas the world of *Incognita* is courtly as well as comic. There is no character even remotely "bad" in it, except nameless ruffians who make the most casual appearance. Only the mildest and most benevolent form of worldly self-seeking is met with, in the persons of the fathers of Aurelian and

Incognita, who want them to marry in order to reconcile the estranged families. These "grave Signiors" (an echo of *Othello*?) are treated with Congreve's blandest irony. The paternal affection of Aurelian's father expresses itself in that he "has been observ'd to have fix'd his eyes upon Aurelian, when much Company has been at Table, and have wept through Earnestness of Intention, if nothing hapned to divert the Object" (p. 35). The fathers are stuffy and inefficient and need to be jollied into behaving sensibly, as when the Duke "rallies" them into a final decision to let the marriage take place by first waiting "till the Wine had taken the effect proposed" and then flattering their children (p. 66). And these manageable old men present the nearest approach to practical cynicism in the book. Obviously the only "probable Casualties" that could complicate life in such a paradise are mistake and misunderstanding.

There is no reason whatsoever for the principal complication, the young men's continued use of each other's identities;[2] but the intricate logic with which everything then hinges upon this absurdity is impeccable. Once the basic absurdity is accepted, the insubstantial-looking edifice of cross-purposes and misunderstandings turns out to be unexpectedly solid. Its collapse is always prevented by some superbly improbable "Casualty" which seems at first unmotivated but which turns out to be what almost amounts to a rational consequence of some other "obstacle." The whole is not as frail as it looks. Why, for example, does not Incognita tell Aurelian her real name even when they agree to marry? Simply (p. 86) because she knows him as Hippolito, and knows that Hippolito is Aurelian's friend (another of those items that have been diffused like air, following Don Fabio's discovery to the Duke), so that she is afraid that if he finds out that she is the Juliana promised to his friend he may refuse to marry her out of the sort of high point of honour which created so many *précieux* dilemmas in the plays of the period (cf. V:iii below). Perfectly straightforward, really.

The linking of this kind of cause and effect shapes itself into a web or lace rather than into a chain. Connections branch out and proliferate in unexpected directions, and they are often purely ornamental: that is to say, they go beyond the practical "Unity of Contrivance" which Congreve describes in the Preface. Leonora's Cousin Lorenzo, for example, is a pleasantly blatant structural device, never as it were on stage, but connected with everything. The duel in which he has been wounded, enabling Hippolito to be mistaken for him at the ball, is the means of bringing Leonora and Hippolito together, but it is also

---

[2] On the low level of motivation native to the romance tradition, see Mish, "English Short Fiction," p. 238; and S. L. Wolff, *The Greek Romances in Elizabethan Prose Fiction* (New York, 1912), passim.

connected with the other couple: it was fought in the quarrel between Aurelian's and Juliana's families (there are many other similarly non-functional links between the two separate courtships). The supreme stroke of economy is the usefulness of Lorenzo's death from this same wound (and the fact that he has to die probably explains why Congreve never lets him out of the wings while still alive). When Leonora's father enters the convent next door to his own garden in order to pray for the soul of "the same Lorenzo so often mentioned" (p. 77), now sinking, he not only leaves Leonora alone in the garden so that Hippolito may overhear her complaining of her "misplaced" love for him, but also establishes the presence of such a convent, making it natural, if that is the right word, that a monk should a little later be at hand to marry the young couple. Nothing is merely accidental in this tissue of coincidence. The sense in which such a plot is "traditionally" artificial, as I called it above, will be examined in the next section.

ii. Background 1: The World of Romance

In a way, it seems surprising that Congreve managed to write a "novel" at all. He was no innovator, and yet too late and too critical to make a straightforward use of the old tidy kind of story, the kind that Boccaccio and Sidney and Malory had used. Different as these older writers are, and not least different with regard to neatness of structure, there is a sense in which they all write tidy stories. A radically different kind of story begins to be written only in the eighteenth century.

The Greek erotic romance of the third and fourth centuries A. D., which was the most important single influence on the seventeenth-century romances, is the simplest example of the quality I mean, precisely because it is notoriously untidy in every other way.[3] Not only are many separate stories interwoven in these romances, in what has become known as the tapestry technique, but they are also full of short, loose threads, and of separate little subplots like loops in the weave; things that are there for their supposed intrinsic interest or beauty or testimony to the author's skill in handling an old theme, not for the sake of any connection with events and characters in the rest of the work. Wolff has analysed the way the love of the picturesque and of the surprising vitiates relevance and loosens the bond of causation in the Greek romance: "In fact, the Alexandrian liked the parts better than the whole, and lingered to elaborate

---

[3] A most helpful analysis of this ancestor of the later romance is provided by S. L. Wolff: see previous note.

whatever pleased." And what pleased the Alexandrian retained its powers to charm for many centuries:

> ... glittering disputations, or antithetical letters and monologues; set-pieces of rhetorical pyrotechny; descriptions of paintings, statues, jewels, utensils, gardens and the like; narratives of local mythology, tales of marvellous beasts—puerile accounts of the phoenix and his pious son, of the elephant's sweet breath, and the terrifying aspect of the giraffe—with much other "unnatural natural history."[4]

Nevertheless, there is an obvious sense in which these stories are "tidy" compared to a modern novel: they are rambling, but they ramble in an orderly world. Sidney's *Arcadia* is a true Alexandrian romance in this respect. Its "Asia" seems small and easily surveyed, like a village. The same people meet again and again, gossip spreads all over it instantly: people with remarkable qualities, such as a particularly brave knight or unchaste woman, become famous for these qualities in "all Asia." How? This cosy ease of communication does more than the supernatural elements to make the world of romance miraculous.

The world of romance is basically the same in both the Greek and the medieval romance, as well as in the gaudy late flowering of the genre in seventeenth-century France. The atmosphere and the furniture vary, to be sure, and the light falls differently; but they are tidy in the same way. Nothing insignificant happens in them. Events are either surprising and wonderful in themselves, or lead to something which is. If a maid in Malory's works bathes in a fountain in the middle of the forest, we know that at least one knight will happen to pass by and be struck by her beauty. If his vizor is down he will certainly turn out to be an old acquaintance, or a woman. No maid just bathes and gets out and dries herself and goes away, no knight has his vizor down for merely personal reasons, such as to hide from his enemies. It means something or leads to something, otherwise it would not be recorded.

The neat, managed quality is quite as conspicuous in the French romances of the seventeenth century as in the earlier types. The miraculous in the sense of the supernatural (giants and enchanted castles) or merely unnatural (heroes who slay ten thousand singlehanded) was by then out of fashion in the romance—heroic unnaturalness still flourished in the English heroic plays, however—although this is somewhat obscured by the continued fashion for declaring in one's preface that it is now time to abandon such doings.[5] Perhaps the purpose of these remarks was to distract attention from the fact that while the long romance was still being written in France (that is, up to about 1660)

---

[4] *The Greek Romances*, p. 6.
[5] See Magendie, *Le Roman français*, pp. 133, 140–57.

its world continued to be managed by the puppet-master of the Greek romances, with his hairbreadth coincidences and visible strings; and such a puppet-master was much more basic to its miraculousness than the outer frills of giants and monsters. This is perceived and explained with great astuteness in the sarcastic account of Charles Sorel in 1671.[6] Sorel despises the romance-writers, who believe themselves to be "dans une grande vraysemblance" because they avoid the most obvious errors of the old pastoral and chivalric romances, and introduce neither miracles nor magic. Their belief is mistaken, because the arm of Fortune in their work is still as long as in *Amadis*:

> N'est-ce pas aussi une chose estrange de raconter qu'en mesme temps dans toutes les parties du Monde tous les Rois ayent des fils & des filles à marier, qui soient amoureux les uns des autres, & qui estans éloignez de leur païs par diverses fortunes, se rencontrent en divers lieux, tantost icy & tantost là, jusques à ce qu'ils soient tous assemblez en mesme endroit pour mettre fin à leur travaux estans tous mariez en un mesme jour? L'une des grandes pieces de ces Romans est encore la reconnoissance de ceux qui ont esté absens l'un de l'autre, ou qui estans proches parens ne s'estoient pourtant jamais veus; Là les Freres retrovent leur Sœurs, & les peres reconnoissent leurs fils & leurs filles, & il se voit que la pluspart de ces Heros sont des Enfans trouvez.[...] Ne sçait on pas que les Autheurs des Romans disposent tout cela comme ils veulent, & qu'ils font de leurs personnages comme les Basteleux de leurs Marionettes, qu'ils tiennent par un fil derriere la toille, faisant tantost parestre les unes & tantost les autres, & faisant qu'elles se rencontrent diversement à leur plaisir?[7]

The vicissitudes of royal foundlings among pirates and sultans had had an extraordinarily long literary lifespan: but by 1671 the contempt of Sorel was far from being so new and daring as he liked to imply (cf. II:i above). As we have seen, the long romances were no longer being written on a literate level in France at this date, nor read by the fashionable. In England, where they had never become really acclimatized,[8] there were only occasional sports like Boyle's *Parthenissa*. But the shorter forms which replaced the romance in the late seventeenth century still move in an ordered and managed world, even if it is not so much one of shipwreck and child-exposure. In the sense described above, the world of the novel was a romance world still.

Ian Watt has described how in the eighteenth century the event that merely happened, without being either extraordinary in itself or leading to anything significant, began to be recorded in literature. In the works of Defoe and Richardson, for the first time, "we feel that the writer's exclusive aim is to

---

[6] Cf. Dorothy Dallas, *Le Roman français de 1660 à 1680*, pp. 36–37.

[7] *De la connoissance des bons livres* (Paris, 1671), pp. 115–17.

[8] On the long romance in England, see Thomas P. Haviland, *The Roman de Longue Haleine on English Soil* (Philadelphia, 1931).

make the words bring his object home to us in all its concrete particularity."[9] If this is characteristic of "the novel," seventeenth-century writers like Aphra Behn obviously did not write "novels." Her stories are set in places called London or Portugal, not Arcadia, but they really happen in the old unlocalized romance world, small, neat and miraculous. Her Oroonoko is brought from "Africa" to a so-called American plantation where he is not required to do any work, although a slave, and where his beloved Imoinda, the African princess, does not surprise the most naive reader by turning up too. This story is obviously of what I called the old tidy kind, with the old kind of stylized, meaningful and patterned events. Aphra Behn's vulgarization of the old miracles[10] is progress, of a kind, but it does not bring them closer to the other kind of story, the kind which admits the pointless and chaotic.

Defoe is an intermediate writer. *Moll Flanders* has many events that just happen, and characters who drift away uninterestingly; most of Moll's children, for example. "By him I had two children" is all we hear of them: it is understood that these children will not turn up like the lost princes and princesses that Sorel complained about. But there are *also* wonderful coincidences, where new characters turn out to have actually been Moll's brother or son all the time. Strictly speaking, all fiction is necessarily more or less mixed in this way: purely "tidy" and purely "chaotic" fiction are both impossible. A modern reader receives the impression that the romances and the early novels are entirely made up of pre-picked significant items, but that is an illusion of perspective. Certainly there is realistic—that is, pointless—detail in *Oroonoko* if one looks for it hard enough; yet the story seems to be completely lacking in what Watt calls the texture of daily life, in concreteness.

The nature of this texture may be clarified by an appeal to Harry Levin's analysis of the nature of realism.[11] Levin sees realism as the technique of systematic disillusionment. That is to say that realism is dependent on the pre-existence of "romance," in the sense of literature which is coming to be felt as old-fashioned, limited and untrue to actual experience. Realism is the opposite of romance, but not because it is "true" to this actual experience, to life, since after all life and literature are different kinds of things. Rather, it gives the illusion of superior truth by unmasking, exploding, showing up, the illusions of earlier literature—"romance"—thereby fatally labelling it "literature" and claiming on its own behalf that "this is not literature but life itself." Such a technique is common to *Madame Bovary* and *Don Quijote*, and the latter is seen by Levin as the decisive influence on European realistic literature.

[9] Ian Watt, *The Rise of the Novel* (1957; rpt. London: Pelican Books, 1972), p. 32.
[10] Cf. Haviland, *The Roman de Longue Haleine*, p. 153.
[11] Harry Levin, *The Gates of Horn: A Study of Five French Realists* (New York, 1966), pp. 24–83.

Turning Levin's analysis around back to front, we might say that although the romantic, distant, "untrue" impression which seventeenth-century fiction makes on us is largely due to the fitfulness of realistic detail and description in this fiction, yet the illusion that these thing are not only fitful but absent is dependent on the post-existence of realism. Or rather, of several realisms; the series of revolutions whereby one generation's realism has become the next generation's romance and then been unmasked in its turn by a new realism makes us see older literature through a sort of reversed Levin effect: "this has nothing to do with life." No doubt this effect of perspective has coloured and simplified my account of "the old tidy kind of story." Nevertheless, and taking this reservation into account, the phrase does seem to cover a reality.

iii. Background 2: The Happy Mistake

I began this chapter by pointing out that the tidiness of the *world* of romance may be studied in its purity, so to speak, in the French seventeenth-century romances, as well as in the early Greek romances, precisely because with respect to what one usually means by structure, these works are so notably *not* tidy, not "well constructed." Unity of contrivance, as Congreve expressively phrased it in his Preface, was theoretically admired, but in practice usually replaced by a shapeless paratactic addition of episodes. "C'est le remplissage qui gâte le plus les romans," writes Magendie in his comprehensive survey of the years 1620—50:

> Tout est bon à leurs auteurs pour allonger l'ouvrage. Ce sont d'abord des aventures oiseuses, parce qu'elles sont sans effet sur la suite des événements. Prisonniers dans une île des Canaries, Cléomède et Méléager complotent de s'enfuir sur un bateau. Cette tentative échoue, le roi du pays ayant soupçonné leur intention. Cependant, c'est avec un navire qu'ils parviendront à se sauver; pourquoi donc avoir imaginé la première entreprise, sinon pour garnir tant bien que mal une centaine de pages?[12]

The most prestigious and highbrow fiction of the seventeenth century, however, aims at being well constructed. To a great extent, this is merely another of the obligatory prefatorial gestures; but *Ibrahim* and *Cassandre* are indeed constructed with the syntactic economy[13] Georges de Scudéry describes in the preface to *Ibrahim*, which is a great feat, considering the length of these works. When the dominant fictional form became shorter, after 1660, economical structure became easier and more commonly realized. The ten-

---

[12] *Le Roman français*, p. 450; the episode referred to occurs in the *Histoire africaine*, II, 196 ff., 260 ff.

[13] Cf. Magendie, *Le Roman français*, p. 449.

dency, then, is towards greater, not less, neatness in fiction at this time. The popular Italian novella is unprecedentedly "plotty," to use Mish's term; and the delight in this kind of plot is shown by the greater popularity of the plotty novels of Cervantes, compared to his simpler realistic ones without amazing coincidences (cf. p. 16 above). Unity of plot is the opposite of the Gothic ramble of the older and most of the newer romances; but it may also be regarded as a further development of the kind of tidiness which the older stories so eminently possess: the providential organization which assigns consequences to everything that happens, so that no bathing maid is ever disappointed of an audience. *Something* reasonably dramatic and interesting will ensue: perhaps she may be espied from one side by a satyr who wants to rape her and from the other by a knight who will rescue her. On the other hand, it is quite likely that in the life of the knight, if he is the hero, the episode is just a digression, an interruption of his quest, or one of a string of adventures which have no connection with one another.

In *Ibrahim* (1641) Madeleine de Scudéry added such a connection. Her brother Georges explained the principle of its construction in the preface:

It is not because the Episodes in the one, and the severall Histories in the other, are not rather beauties, than defects; but it is alwaies necessary, that the adress of him which imployes them should hold them in some sort to this principall action, to the end, that by this ingenious concatenation, all the parts of them should make but one body, and that nothing may be seen in them which is loose and unprofitable. Thus the mariage of my *Justiniano* and his *Isabella*, being the object which I have proposed unto my self, I have imployed all my care so to doe, that all the parts of my work may tend to that conclusion; that there may be a strong connexion between them; and that, except the obstacle which fortune opposeth to the desires of my *Heros,* all things may advance, or at lestwise indeavor to advance his mariage, which is the end of my labor.[14]

Not only the "world," but the plot too, is neat here. Scudéry's idea of neatness is, even so, less radical than Congreve's: everything *except* the obstacles advances the marriage. Congreve's ambition that every obstacle act "as subservient to that purpose, which at first it seems to oppose" (Preface, p. 34) is of course exactly that of the ideally "well-constructed" neo-classical play. "As for the third unity," says Crites in Dryden's *Essay of Dramatic Poesy* (1668), "which is that of action [...] now the poet is to aim at one great and complete action, to the carrying on of which all things in his play, even the very obstacles, are to be subservient."[15] The ingenious way in which the "obstacles" in *Incognita*, caused by excessive foolishness of behaviour, turn

---

[14] *Ibrahim. Or the Illustrious Bassa. An Excellent New Romance*, trans. Henry Cogan (London, 1652), Preface, sig. A3ʳ.
[15] *"Of Dramatic Poesy" and Other Critical Essays*, ed. George Watson (London: Everyman's Library, 1962), I, 29.

out to be the best thing that could have happened is, I hope, to some extent apparent from my summary of the plot. Aubrey Williams sees a religious significance in this insistence on the "lucky mistake," typified by Aurelian's accidental fall in the churchyard, which causes the ruffian's bullet to pass him harmlessly. The reverse of the lucky mistake is the ingenious planning which miscarries and works against the very purpose which the character is labouring for, like the efforts of Aurelian to avoid his destined bride Juliana, actually Incognita, in order to retain his beloved Incognita, actually Juliana:

All such self-defeating contrivances and designs, along with all such happy errors and fortunate mistakes, seem in their turn to point towards certain crucial and highly emblematic situations in which characters are said to be in a "maze" or "at a loss," or (better still) are said to "grope" in the dark or to be "left in the Dark." At such moments "in the Dark," when a character has "wandred into the Dominions of Silence and of Night," there occurs, in a most critical "Instant of Time," an act of Providential design.[16] The effect of such terms and of such situations in the novel is to suggest that amidst all human contrivances, and amidst all human "success" and all human "error," there work the contrivances of Providence, which sees that a kind of "justice" is done.[17]

Williams sees *Incognita*, and also Congreve's plays, as "drawing-room theodicies" (p. 17), as demonstrations of the care of providence, set off by the ironic helplessness of human intention. The hand of God is revealed in the way characters are "frustrated by their own ingenuity and designs or saved by their own seeming limitations or apparent folly or even by their mishaps and stumblings" (pp. 16—17): thus Congreve answers "the basic theodicean questions" put by Aurelian in his exclamation against the cruelty of fate ("Oh ye unequal Powers," etc.).

This interpretation of a basic comic pattern seems too specific. If *Incognita* is a drawing-room theodicy, Wycherley's *Country Wife* is, too, with its far more explicit and pointed treatment of the theme of characters "frustrated by their own ingenuity and designs" (Pinchwife!); and that somehow does not seem right. The combination of frustrated ingenuity and happy mistake is probably the most popular "theme" of farce and comedy of any age, and not necessarily significant of anything beyond itself, as is persuasively suggested by Wolff's analysis of the Greek romances (cf. IV:ii above). These are crammed with "ironies of fate" of this kind, especially of course the good old "bringing about of an event by the very means taken to prevent it," for example bringing about the events presaged by an oracle by exposing an infant

---

[16] This refers to the stumbling of Aurelian in the churchyard, which occurs "just in that Instant of Time when the Villain fired his Pistol" (*Incognita*, p. 71).

[17] "Congreve's *Incognita* and the Contrivances of Providence," p. 9.

in order to avoid these events. Wolff sees this pervasive irony as a special case of that love of paradox and antithesis which characterizes the Alexandrian writers. They delighted in contrasts, and these extreme contrasts between intention and result "possess an intenser, a more concentrated flavor, as it were, than [others]. An event the occurrence of which has merely not been expected, is less piquant than an event which has actively been designed *not* to occur."[18] This degeneracy of tragic irony into piquancy is in full force in seventeenth-century fiction and drama too, as may be expected from the fatal attraction which rhetorical antithesis as an elegancy of style still had. The power-mad Providence visualized by Williams shows exactly the same sadistically benevolent sense of humour as that which presides over Dryden's or Wycherley's comedies: Dryden stresses its benevolence, that is, the fortunate results of an imbecile lack of forethought in his young hotheaded heroes, while Wycherley stresses its sadism, that is, the disasters to themselves which follow the best efforts of clever and calculating villains and stooges.

Aurelian's accusations against fate are too completely conventional to support Williams' argument: "God-huffing," it was called in the tragedies,[19] and absolutely obligatory in Aurelian's situation (cf. V:iii below). That is not to say that such accusations are not "theodicean," of course; but Congreve does not emerge from a comparison with Restoration drama (comedy and tragedy) as being especially interested in such problems, in the context of his age. It is because *Incognita* is so intricately unified that the paradoxical pattern is unusually conspicuous in it: the obstacles are never merely obstacles, because that would be uneconomical and also less comic; they are advances too. Conversely, the ingenious designs never succeed, both because that would be less comic, and because, if one did, the plot would collapse.

iv. Functionalism

What I have said about the intricate unity of *Incognita* is not intended to imply that absolutely every detail in it carries the plot forward: it would have been impossible to summarize it at all if that had been the case. *Incognita* is fifty pages long in Norman Jeffares' edition (in which *The Way of the World* takes up ninety pages): much shorter than a modern novel, but still longer than an ordinary short story. Obviously the plot is decorated and diversified with such things as descriptions and conversations. The witty conversation between Aurelian and Incognita at the ball is no necessary part of the whole, for

---

[18] *The Greek Romances*, p. 214.
[19] See David S. Berkeley, "The Art of 'Whining' Love," *SP*, 52 (1955), 478–96.

instance, but then it *is* witty: it justifies itself. *Incognita* is entirely functional, just like the romances; it contains only the interesting and the necessary. If a descriptive detail or an event is neither witty nor splendid nor amazing, the reader may, and does, assume that it will turn out to be necessary instead: that is, a necessary part of a larger whole which has at least some of these interesting qualities. The business of procuring Cousin Lorenzo's "habit" for Hippolito is a typical incident of this kind (pp. 38—39). It lacks immediate entertainment value so conspicuously that it proclaims its necessity at once: obviously, the reader feels, this is the beginning of somebody's being mistaken for somebody else because of the clothes he wears. Everything in the book has a reason for being there which is both good and obvious. The description of the looks and apparel of the characters is more extreme in its functionalism than is that of the *milieu*: the "Florence" of *Incognita* is permitted an occasional unfunctional dab of local colour.[20]

The only details of dress which are conceived to be decorative and/or significant enough to justify themselves, that is, to be interesting although not necessary to the story, are two imports from, respectively, romance and comedy: the colours of the suits of armour for the tilting (see below, V:iii) and the sexily informal dress of the heroines at the high points of the action (see below, V:i). What is worn on other occasions, both by the principals and by the various gay companies, Congreve ignores; or rather he deliberately skips it, showing at the same time his awareness that he is excluding something which is usually included and considered a beauty. Thus the ordinary "fine" clothes of the spectators at the tilting are too banal a subject for him, so he lazily recommends the reader to dress them "in what is most agreeable to his own Fancy," merely assuring him that "they were all very Fine and very Glorious" (p. 63).

Congreve draws attention to how extreme his niggardliness of concrete particularity is when he points out that he is *not* going to describe the dress of Incognita at the ball, as the reader may be presumed to expect, and gives an elegantly teasing reason: "I should by right now describe her Dress, which was extreamly agreeable and rich, but 'tis possible I might err in some material Pin or other, in the sticking of which may be the whole grace of the Drapery depended" (pp. 43—44). As usual, he is all the more ready with his general, unvisualized praise: of course the dress was extremely agreeable and rich. Perhaps the most striking instance of Congreve's idiosyncracy against describing clothes is the high level of abstraction on which Aurelian and Incognita at

---

[20] For these touches, Congreve used John Raymond's *An Itinerary Contayning a Voyage Made through Italy, in the Yeare 1646 and 1647*; see E. S. de Beer, "Congreve's *Incognita*, the Source of its Setting, with a Note on Wilson's *Belphegor*," *RES*, 8 (1932), 74—77.

the ball discuss philosophical and psychological aspects of dress, and draw examples from the people around them, without ever mentioning such a thing as a colour or a particular garment (pp. 41—43).

When a garment is an important prop, such as the "habit" of Cousin Lorenzo, which is worn first by Hippolito at the ball and then by his governor, it is indeed described; but only exactly so far as is necessary for its function in the plot. The importance of Lorenzo's suit is that first Leonora mistakes Hippolito dressed in it for Lorenzo, and then Aurelian thinks that the governor, who has borrowed it after Hippolito's return from the ball in order to go back himself and have some fun, is Hippolito; while the men who attack the governor in the street, being former servants of the man Lorenzo had killed in that duel which estranged the families of Juliana-Incognita and Aurelian, had taken him for Lorenzo. The suit is to *Incognita* as Desdemona's handkerchief is to *Othello*, only in a more complicated and interconnected way; but the last thing Congreve displays is an interest in bringing it "home to us in all its concrete particularity" (cf. pp. 53—54 above), the kind of interest which is so memorably seen in Richardson's careful visualization of the piquantly simple clothes Pamela puts on to leave Mr. B:s house. When aspects of the appearance of Lorenzo's habit are mentioned, it is always merely because practical considerations require these particular qualities. Thus it is "as fit for Hippolito as if it had been made for him"(p. 39); very necessary, since otherwise he would not have worn it. It has diamond buttons on the sleeves: Aurelian sees them glimmer in the dark street when the governor is wearing it, and jumps to the conclusion that the person being attacked is Hippolito (it is only at this late point that the existence of the buttons is mentioned). That is all.

The praise accorded to the human form is as abstract as the "rich," "glorious," "fine," applied to clothes; it is more elaborate but no more particular. The reader is not in the least encouraged to form an idea of what the main characters look like: they are all young and beautiful, and Incognita is taller than Leonora. This last has a special function: Hippolito hopes for a moment that the lady who visits their chamber "close veil'd" (p. 68) is Leonora, but then he perceives that she has "much the Advantage in Stature of his Mistress"; in fact, it is Incognita, looking for Aurelian. That, again, is all: as so often in the romances, we do not even know whether they are fair or dark. The "description" of Incognita mentions no details at all. It is instead a learned and antithetic elaboration of the simple theme of beauty:

One might have seen something in her Composition resembling the Formation of Epicurus his World, as if every Atome of Beauty had concurr'd to unite an excellency. Had that curious Painter lived in her days, he might have avoided his painful search, when he collected from the choicest pieces the most choice Features, and by a due Disposition and Judicious Symmetry of those exquisite parts, made one whole and perfect Venus. Nature seem'd here to have play'd the Plagiary, and to have molded into Substance the most refined Thoughts of inspired Poets. Her Eyes diffus'd Rays comfortable as warmth and piercing as the light; they would have worked a passage through the straightest Pores, and with a delicious heat, have play'd about the most obdurate frozen Heart, untill 'twere melted down to Love. Such Majesty and Affability were in her Looks: so alluring, yet commanding was her Presence, that it mingled awe with love; kindling a Flame which trembled to aspire. She had danced much, which, together with her being close masked, gave her a tincture of Carnation more than ordinary. (pp. 51—52)

Apart from the charming touch of the last sentence, the "beauty" of the heroine is simply a given factor, a counter to play with.

In the episode of the tournament, which I shall try to place in its perspective in the next chapter (V:iii), female beauty becomes still more rarefied and abstract: that of Donna Catharina is blandly assumed to be directly proportionate to her social position, without any reference to her actual looks:

... two Cavaliers undertook to defend the Beauty of Donna Catharina, against all who would not allow her preheminence of their Mistresses. This thing was only designed for show and form, none presuming that any body would put so great an affront upon the Bride and Duke's Kinswoman, as to dispute her pretensions to the first place in the Court of Venus. (p. 63)

In fact, nobody is so rude as to dispute these pretensions except the strangers Aurelian and Hippolito, and they only do it because they mistake the Duke's kinswoman for an ordinary lady, and are "much concerned for their mistake" when it is pointed out to them.

"Much of the description in the courtly tradition," writes Muscatine in *Chaucer and the French Tradition*, "is static and formal. It is often chosen not for direct use in the dramatic action, but for ulterior significance, which can range from the generally atmospheric to the most minutely allegorical."[21] The romance, Greek, medieval or heroic, is, by a characteristic paradox, conspicuous not only for the functional way in which one event leads to another, but also for its large tracts of static and decorative description. Descriptive detail is characteristic of the old tidy kind of story because it is a special, "romantic" kind of detail that is described: tournaments and feasts, hunts and armings, mottoes and devices. Practically useless, such events and objects are all the more heavily significant on other levels, laden with symbolism. The tournament in *Incognita* partakes of this quality; it does not lead to anything to speak of, since its only plot function is to allow Aurelian's father to espy him from the audience, and thus to let him know that his son is in town: an effect which could very easily have been arranged without so much circum-

[21] P. 17.

stance. The episode is blatantly ornamental and at the same time emblematic, as I will try to show later.

The reason which everything in *Incognita* has for being there is not necessarily always so easy to define as in the case of the simple examples I have given: but in the experience of reading the book, each item radiates a feeling of selectness, and an assurance that the reason for it will be found if the reader cares to take the context apart. A feeling, in other words, that this is a tidy world. The principle is the reverse of that which operates in *Pamela*, and the effect is the reverse too. For the reader of *Incognita* there can be no involvement: he need not exert himself to gather meaning, to "participate" in the way which Ian Watt in his discussion of *Pamela* describes as characteristic of the realistic novel:

> The very lack of selectiveness, indeed, impels us to a more active involvement in the events and feelings described: we have to pick significant items of character and behaviour out of a wealth of circumambient detail, much as in real life we attempt to gather meaning from the casual flux of circumstance. This is the kind of participation which the novel typically induces: it makes us feel that we are in contact not with literature but with the raw materials of life itself as they are momentarily reflected in the minds of the protagonists.[22]

Incognita makes us feel that we are in contact with an artefact as far removed from the raw materials of life as possible. So far, this is nothing peculiar to *Incognita*: it is the feeling which the old, neat pre-novel kind of story typically induces, with its predictable surprisingness. Moreover, as we have seen, the kind of plot which *Incognita* has, the plot of amazing coincidences and turns of fortune, was characteristic of a very fashionable genre in the later seventeenth century: the "plotty" Italian-type novella, which was very much neater still than the typical romance in providing connections, causes and consequences.

What *is* peculiar to *Incognita* (though not necessarily unique, of course) is that it takes these various kinds of neatness further still, and extends this quality until it becomes a parody of itself, as I will try to show.

v. Facetious Structure

I must return for a moment to the argument of an earlier chapter, where I quoted a passage from Sidney's *Arcadia* (p. 46 above) in order to illustrate the difference between Sidney's devotion to parallelism and antithesis and Con-

---

[22] *The Rise of the Novel*, p. 219.

greve's more informal and natural—though not colloquial—style. My point was that Sidney's language, in the words of Greg and Waith, serves as a basis of composition: that is, it is of a piece with the situations he describes; whereas Congreve's easy language is the vehicle of a plot which is as formal and rhetorical as that of the *Arcadia*.

My chapter headings "Style" and "Structure" are admittedly more convenient than correct. Of course style and structure are not independent entities: Congreve's style is as integral to his method as a whole as Sidney's. What I have so far discussed in the present chapter is not so much the structure of the book as a whole, but rather the structure of the "world" of *Incognita*, the structure of its events. That the structure of the book is inseparable from its style is shown very concretely by the way my natural wish to put a passage from *Incognita* beside the quotation from *Arcadia*, so as to compare their different stylistic handling of similar arguments, was thwarted. There *is* no passage in *Incognita* that can be used for such a neat demonstration, since there is no passage that sets forth the stylized and formal situation in which the lovers find themselves. Congreve never describes that situation at all, never elaborates on the contrasts and parallelisms of his plot in the way Sidney, following the Alexandrian writers with their fondness for "the surprising," does on practically every page of both the "new" and the "old" *Arcadia*. The plot of *Incognita*, with all its symmetry, merely unfolds itself, without any insistence on its pattern, without any running recapitulations to underline it.

Instead of insistence and recapitulation, Congreve has his own understated way of emphasizing his pattern. He does this by means of little details, dropped into place with all the carefully studied carelessness of a Restoration gentleman's morning *déshabillé*. These details are more conspicuous in the texture of the novel than impressive in the enumeration. The functionalism which I have just described, only the necessary or witty or beautiful being admitted, means that any apparently unfunctional detail is very noticeable against the general spareness. This is probably the reason why critics who write about the romances often become very irritated at their absurdities and contradictions and the unmotivated behaviour of their heroes.[23] These things are so conspicuous because everything is conspicuous in radically selective writing. The romances are full of absurdities and of poor motivation, but so is *Pamela*, surely, and yet it does not usually annoy readers in that particular way. Richardson needs unreasonable and illogical behaviour in his characters to prevent his plot from falling apart, just as the romancers do; but in *Pamela*, the naked lack of motivation for certain actions is blurred by a convincing,

---

[23] See for example Magendie, *Le Roman français*, p. 206.

lifelike chaos of inconsequential data. In it, or in any other "modern" novel, the details which pick up and exaggerate the symmetry in *Incognita* would be so overwhelmed by the "circumambient detail" of which Watt writes as to become invisible. It seems politic to point out that in *Incognita* the spareness of texture does make these significant details reasonably striking, before I begin actually to cite instances.

Congreve is not content with the intricate economy of cause and effect which I described above (IV:i), and which is surely adequately overdone in itself. He tinges the neatness of his story with absurdity by extending it into pure, non-causal, ornamental symmetry. It is obvious enough even from my summary of the plot that the motif of the mixed-up identities is reinforced by parallels between the adventures of the two heroes, and between their two courtships. Moreover, the similarity between Aurelian and Hippolito in character and even in looks is stressed.[24] Of course characters in the same general category, in this case that of amiable young men, are in seventeenth-century novels often, not to say usually, indistinguishable merely because they are only stereotypes. Aurelian and Hippolito have this kind of similarity, certainly: they are both everything they ought to be, like Sidney's Musidorus and Pyrocles. They are handsome, susceptible, clever, and good at feats of arms. But they are *meant* to be alike as well. Hippolito "had so wrought himself into the Affections of Aurelian, through a Conformity of Temper, an Equality of Years, and something of resemblance in Feature and Proportion, that he look'd upon him as his second self" (p. 36). The shift from affection to identity here is rather odd. It is in itself commonplace to describe the friendship in terms of Hippolito being Aurelian's "second self";[25] but what kind of a reason is a "resemblance in Feature and Proportions" for "Affections"? Moreover, the commonplace is very exact here: Aurelian is as it were the primary hero, Hippolito a sort of auxiliary or echo, whose concerns are described much more briefly. Thus there is a full-dress, laboured and "conceited" account (which I quote above) of the impression Incognita's beauty makes on Aurelian when she pulls off her mask for a moment at the ball, while Leonora in exactly the same situation vis-à-vis Hippolito merely discovers to him "the most Angelick Face that he had ever beheld" (p. 45) and that is that. Of course this feature is not original; several of Cervantes' *Novelas Ejemplares*, for example, have as heroes two friends with similar but not equally important adventures.

Towards the end of the book, the comedy of errors seems to have confused

---

[24] Cf. Maximillian E. Novak, "Congreve's *Incognita* and the Art of the Novella," p. 335, n. 13.
[25] See for example Joseph Kepple's *Maiden-Head Lost by Moon-Light*, in *Restoration Prose Fiction*, ed. Charles C. Mish (Lincoln, 1970), p. 170.

Congreve himself for a moment into a disconcerting double-exposure effect with regard to his heroes: who is who? Leonora's illogical or superlogical reaction upon being told Hippolito's real name after their marriage suggests actual interchangeability:

> She was under some concern at first to find that she was still mistaken [the first time was in taking him for Cousin Lorenzo]; but his Behaviour, and the Reasons he gave, soon reconciled him to her; his Person was altogether as agreeable, his Estate and Quality not at all inferiour to Aurelian's. (p. 84)

(Of course she has never seen the real Aurelian.) It makes sense, certainly, for her to compare Hippolito's actual estate and quality with what she had thought he had, as Aurelian, and to find that the comparison is not to the disadvantage of his present equipment in these respects. But she also seems to be comparing his "person," that is, his appearance, with what it was when she thought he was Aurelian, and concluding that he is quite as handsome now. It is as if the face of the man she has just married had transformed itself too, along with his worldly status, at the moment when he confessed the imposition: a confusion which could hardly happen in a realistic novel, where the reader is always encouraged to form a picture in his mind's eye of what the main characters look like.

An earlier remark by Congreve implies something perhaps equally odd: when the heroes enter the ballroom where they will soon set eyes on the heroines for the first time, they are described as gaining the favorable opinion of the ladies there by having "something inexpressibly pleasing in their Air and Mien, different from other People, and indeed differing from one another" (p. 40). Why not? Is there really any need to tell the reader that their air and mien are not the same? Note the "indeed"; it would be strange if they *were* the same, surely, but Congreve is suggesting that the strangeness is on the other side.

This peculiar underlining of the similarity between the heroes' "persons" is matched by the typically off-hand and at the same time conspicuous way in which Congreve urges the parallels between their activities on the reader's attention. He specifies that

> By Computation now (which is a very remarkable Circumstance) Hippolito entred this Garden near upon the same Instant, when Aurelian wandred into the old Monastery and found his Incognita in Distress. (p. 78)

The relation of *Incognita* to the Restoration stage is discussed in the next chapter; but it may be remarked here that the dance-like symmetry of movement indicated in this passage is similar (only still more gratuitous) to the "patterned behaviour" of Restoration tragedy described by Clifford Leech:

... we can find many similar scenes in Restoration tragedy. In Sir Robert Howard's *The Indian Queen*, which Dryden helped to write, the queen Zempoalla and her general Traxalla are respectively in love with their captives Montezuma and Orazia, who love one another: in IV.i the four of them are on the stage, which represents a prison: at first Zempoalla is about to kill Orazia, and Traxalla about to kill Montezuma: neither dares to accomplish the deed lest the other should follow suit: then suddenly there is a change of places, Zempoalla gets between Traxalla and Montezuma, ready to defend Montezuma's life, and Traxalla is then in front of Orazia, whom he is ready to defend: this, of course, is as much an impasse as the preceding situation. The scene does not advance the plot, it is merely an occasion for patterned movement and patterned speech.[26]

The antithetic and rhetorical spirit of Sidney's Pyrocles lived on, only slightly muted, in Restoration tragedy. Congreve's formalized situation in *Incognita*, on the other hand, is thrown off without any patterned speech: it is not the occasion of anything, it is simply there. Certainly, as Leech points out, "an audience accustomed to this kind of patterned behaviour sees it very differently from the private reader." Moreover, the stage—at least, the Restoration stage—is of course incapable of representing actions in different localities as simultaneous, and so could not easily make a pattern out of causally *un*connected events, as Congreve is doing is the passage quoted: he goes one better, with this purely ornamental pirouette. There is no practical connection at all between the activities of Aurelian and Hippolito at the moment in question. On the other hand, each is about to meet, accidentally, a fetchingly and unconventionally dressed mistress in a secluded, though urban, spot out of doors and persuade her into marriage, which is surely almost too coincidental in itself, so why not push it over the edge by letting them do it "near upon the same Instant"? It is not even a particularly remarkable circumstance, really, compared to many of the circumstances that are necessary to avoid a premature eclaircissement.

It is perhaps a heavy description of such an effect to suggest that when Congreve points out how "remarkable" a random and superfluous little piece of coincidence is, he is "commenting" on the stylized tidiness of his plot. His little parenthesis about the very remarkable circumstance, read in the context of a dizzy but silently accepted structure of coincidences, some of them much more than remarkable, is a kind of romantic irony: a phenomenon which is not in itself unusual in the more sophisticated seventeenth-century fiction. Touches of self-parody can be found in the later romances, even in those that represent most completely the concept of "romance" in Levin's sense: *Ibrahim*, or

---

[26] Clifford Leech, "Restoration Tragedy: A Reconsideration," *Durham University Journal*, 11 (1950), rpt. in *Restoration Drama: Modern Essays in Criticism*, ed. John Loftis (New York, 1966), pp. 152–53.

Parthenissa. The romance writers are quite likely to remark, in the middle of some unlikely story, that if this were a romance, now, I would here provide a verbatim letter, or a description of arms and mottoes, but since it is merely a plain blunt true story, I must dispense with such beauties (cf. II:ii above). Such asides are a more sophisticated expression of the embarrassment which prompted the pathetically clumsy attempts to explain the retention of letters and the overhearing of conversations which I quoted above (pp. 30–31). *Ibrahim* is no more realistic than *Astrée*, but it shows an awareness of the absurdities of its own conventions: conventions which at the time of *Astrée* were taken for granted and elaborated as being the proper ornaments of the genre. This awareness in *Ibrahim* is especially connected with the witty and jovial figure of "the French Marquis," who tells his friends many "histories," and who can for instance say of a letter which crops up in one of them:

If I had as happy a memory as a *Romanzes Heros*, I would recite it unto you without changing a sillable, but since I have it not, it shall suffice that I do tell you in generall, ... [27]

The length of these histories was another source of embarrassment. They must have taken days to tell, and what about food and drink and sleep, and patience, for the tellers and the listeners?[28] The sarcastic French Marquis is interested in that problem too. He announces his "Third History" with a special headline on the page to set it off typographically, in the usual manner, and with "all the ceremonies of a man that prepares himself for a long Narration": and then reels off his narrative in ten brisk lines. The company laugh delightedly at this wit:

It must be acknowledged said *Leonida* at length, that if they which write our *Romanzes*, did make them deliver their Relations in this sort, we should not admire, as we do, the wonderfull memories of their Heroes, who make narrations, which cause them to pass whole daies without eating, and nights without sleeping.[29]

Haviland writes that in passages like these, *Ibrahim* "naively satirizes the very frailties of which it is composed,"[30] which seems a little harsh. The double-exposure effect of such satire is not necessarily naive. The "reversed Levin effect" which I described above makes it difficult now to realize that the romance-writers did not think of themselves, at least, whatever they might

---

[27] *Ibrahim*, Pt. 2, Bk. 2, p. 29; cf. Haviland, *The Roman de Longue Haleine*, p. 57.
[28] Cf. Magendie, *Le Roman français*: "Parfois, la personne qui parle promet d'être brève; mais cela est rare, et cette engagement demeure théorique. Parfois, elle s'aperçoit qu'elle est 'trop prolixe dans sa narration', ou que son récit 'passe une longeur raisonnable'. Mais comme à ce moment l'histoire est finie, ce n'est là qu'une vaine formule de politesse" (p. 452).
[29] *Ibrahim*, Pt. 2, Bk. 4, pp. 73–74.
[30] *The Roman de Longue Haleine*, p. 52.

think of other romance-writers, as engaged in writing old-fashioned, unreal and fading fiction: they did not think of themselves as providing a foil for future realisms. If the genre seemed stale to an individual writer he improved it as best he could in his own book, although the changes he introduced are likely to be invisible to us. To speak of romance heroes, as the French Marquis does, implicitly setting himself up as a real person, is a device of realism. Absurdly inadequate in the light of the more radical tradition of Cervantes, it may have seemed fresh and convincing in its own tradition. "This is not romance," announce Scudéry and Boyle—yet it *is*, as all the other pages proclaim. The sophistication shown by the incidental self-parody in the romances leads only to irony, not to anything new. These romancers have their cake and eat it too, by the becoming depreciation of conventions they have no idea of renouncing. The same romantic irony can be seen in Restoration comedies, with their disconcerting references to dramatic conventions and stagecraft; like the exclamation of Witwoud upon entering the conventionally crowded stage near the end of *The Way of the World*:

Witwoud. Hey day! what are you all got together like Players at the end of the last Act?[31]

However, Congreve's self-mockery in *Incognita* is on a different level from these little mini-parodies which crop up in romances and plays. It is the whole "world" of *Incognita*, which is the world of romance, that he is commenting on in the passage where he stresses the remarkableness of his little coincidence: for the remarkable coincidence is the very essence of the world of romance. He treats the nub of his plot, the ostensible surprise ending of the story, with the same irony. Even in my summary of the plot, it is of course painfully obvious from the moment Juliana is introduced that Incognita is going to turn out to differ "nothing from Juliana, but in her Name." It is possible to analyse how and where it is made still more clear in the book itself: for example, Congreve's few reticences stand out very conspicuously, since his narrative technique is generally the ordinary seventeenth-century one of omniscience, and since, apart from the occasional assumption of comic ignorance, he therefore enters the minds of his characters whenever they may be supposed to contain anything of interest. In the only glimpse the reader gets of "Juliana" before the dénouement, her father orders her to marry Aurelian in the morning, and teases her fondly about it. How does she respond? "Juliana took her leave of the Company very gravely, as if not much delighted with her Father's Rallery" (p. 67). This external description ("as if"—it is the outside

---

[31] V.i.521—22; all references to Congreve's plays are to *The Complete Plays of William Congreve*, ed. Herbert Davis (Chicago, 1967).

observer speaking) is absurdly suspicious. Of course we recall that "Incognita" happens to have good reason to be grave at such an arrangement, since she is interested in the young man she has just met at the ball, actually Aurelian himself, but known to her as Hippolito.

It is possible to make any number of such points, but the one example I have given is surely enough to show that it would be like deluging the reader with a wealth of commentary to prove that Iago is subtle. None of this detail is required, because the reader—both the modern and the seventeenth-century reader—has already recognized what *kind* of story *Incognita* is: the neat, symmetrical no-loose-ends kind. The only really surprising ending would have been the one that avoided the expected "surprise": one where Incognita turned out on the last page to be somebody called Isabella whom we had heard nothing of before. The only surprise involved in the story as it stands is that Congreve should have thought it worth his while to keep up the pretence that the reader might conceivably *not* have guessed the outcome. He does keep it up, after a fashion, but with a good deal of winking and nudging. The identity of the heroine is shrouded in a mock secrecy which is about as impenetrable as a stage disguise.

In some ways, it seems as if suspense in the detective-story sense, which keeps the reader guessing how it will all come out in the end, was not only unvalued but positively disliked in the seventeenth century. Stories are often adorned with summaries—"arguments"—in the form of long descriptive sub-titles or chapter headings. This is probably the single trait which contributes most to making this fiction strangely and unsympathetically "old" to a modern reader. How could anyone think that a summary is to a story as the eye is to the body?[32] At the same time, there are some intimations that there may have been some development during the seventeenth century towards greater appreciation of the suspense element, at the expense of the joys of knowing in advance, with their attendant opportunities for feeling superior to the characters of the book or play ("dramatic irony"). A characteristic simile in Aphra Behn's *Unfortunate Bride* seems to imply that she shares, and assumes that her readers share, the modern habit of reading "to see what happens":

Women enjoy'd are like Romances read, or Raree-shows once seen, meer Tricks of the slight of Hand, which, when found out, you only wonder at your selves for wondering so before at them. 'Tis Expectation endears the Blessing; Heaven would

---

[32] This was the professed opinion of the Italian translator of Cervantes' *Novelas Ejemplares*, in explanation of his own addition of the summaries which Cervantes had failed to provide: see Esther J. Crooks, "Translations of Cervantes into French," in *Cervantes across the Centuries*, ed. Angel Flores and M. J. Benardete (New York, 1947), p. 295.

not be Heaven, could we tell what 'tis. When the Plot's out you have done with the Play, and when the last Act's done, you see the Curtain drawn with great indifferency.[33]

It is in keeping with the attitude suggested here that she does not provide "arguments" for her own stories. Earlier in the century, Beaumont and Fletcher seem to have exploited the detective-story kind of appeal very deliberately. Or, as the playwright and poet William Cartwright put it in his complimentary verses to their first and second folios:

> None can prevent the Fancy, and see through
> At the first opening; all stand wondring how
> The thing will be untill it is; which thence
> With fresh delights still cheats, still takes the sence.[34]

Their technique for cheating the sense can be startlingly modern. In *The Maid's Tragedy*, "like the writers of detective fiction, [they] deliberately falsify their point of view."[35] The audience is tricked, along with the infatuated husband, into believing Evadne an innocent virgin, right up to the moment on the wedding night when she informs him that she has been the king's mistress. A yet earlier example of a still longer deception is of course Jonson's *Silent Woman*. The technique remained exceptional, however, both in fiction and drama. In the world of romance, as I have insisted above, we know that the consequences of an ordinary event, which is not interesting in itself, must be interesting: that is, must be exceptional, surprising. The surprising, then, not really paradoxically, becomes the predictable. The reader expects to be surprised, and frequently there is only one possible surprising consequence of an action: for a baby which has been committed to the waves, the only exceptional and hence the only possible consequence is that it will survive; and similarly with a lone knight attacked by twenty. When stories move in such a world, the criterion of surprisingness, which was insisted upon by critics, makes them so completely predictable that they do not even need summaries. Take the king's two children, Garinter and Fawnia, in Greene's *Pandosto*: he is brought up at court, she is thrown into the sea. She is obviously much safer than he, for he may die (and does); but she cannot. There is an oracle to make doubly sure, but it is not really necessary: we can work it out without help that she must be her father's heir. A child thrown into the sea not only cannot die, in a romance; it is also sure, by the rule of contrast and irony, to inherit any throne which is anywhere near available to it, and therefore Garinter is doomed.

[33] *Works*, V, 407.
[34] Quoted by Edward M. Wilson, "Cervantes and English Literature of the Seventeenth Century," *Bulletin Hispanique*, 50, No. 1 (1948), 40.
[35] E. M. Waith, *The Pattern of Tragicomedy in Beaumont and Fletcher*, p. 22.

Nevertheless, the criterion of surprisingness *was* insisted upon by critics, and it did have a place. What this place was is suggested by Charlotte Morgan's description of the Greek erotic romances, which were so popular and so widely imitated in the seventeenth century (cf. IV:ii above):

> In the sequence of these episodes no effort is made to develop a central theme. The only attempt to give even the semblance of unity consists in having the final result work out the fulfillment of an oracle, and in having dreams and visions prepare the way for lesser episodes. The desire is to accomplish the result in a manner most surprising to the reader. Surprise and suspense are two of the most striking qualities of the Greek romances, and writers and critics of the seventeenth century insisted upon them as indispensable in a good romance.[36]

The idea is "to accomplish the result *in a manner* most surprising"; the result itself is no surprise, being even foreshadowed by oracles; the suspense lies in seeing how the foreseen will be brought about. The goal is nothing, the road everything. Read in the light of this distinction, the "modern" character of the quotation from Aphra Behn may well be illusory. Although she does not go in for long, summary-type titles to her novels, giving away what, specifically, will happen, she often indicates it as it were generally (what *kind* of thing will happen), in her catchy, curiosity-stirring titles: *The Nun; Or, The Perjur'd Beauty*; *The Unhappy Mistake; Or, The Impious Vow Punish'd*. The subtitle to *Incognita* is of this cat-out-of-the-bag kind too: *Love and Duty Reconcil'd*.

The distinction between the obvious goal and the surprising road underlies this passage in Congreve's Preface to *Incognita*:

> The design of the Novel is obvious, after the first meeting of Aurelian and Hippolito with Incognita and Leonora, and the difficulty is in bringing it to pass, maugre all apparent obstacles, within the compass of two day. How many probable Casualties intervene in opposition to the main Design, *viz.* of marrying two Couple so oddly engaged in an intricate Amour, I leave the Reader at his leisure to consider: . . . (pp. 33–34)

The Oxford English Dictionary gives two main senses for "design": "a mental plan" (French *dessein*) and "a plan in art" (French *dessin*). Congreve's phrase "the design of the Novel" at the beginning of the passage quoted naturally suggests the second of these; but his use of "Design" in the fourth line makes it clear that he is using the word in the sense of *dessein*, specifically in *OED*'s sense 3: "The thing aimed at; the end in view; the final purpose," as in "If Milk be thy Design; with plenteous Hand Bring Clover-grass" (Dryden, *Virg. Georg.* III:604). The obvious design of *Incognita* is that of marrying the two couples; the scope for surprisingness is in how it is "brought to pass."

---

[36] Charlotte E. Morgan, *The Rise of the Novel of Manners: A Study of English Prose Fiction Between 1660 and 1740*, Columbia University Studies in English (New York, 1911), p. 12.

That there should be no secrets, in the sense of a "falsified point of view," from the audience is highly characteristic of Restoration comedy. This is especially so in those plays where much of the humour and meaning comes from the characters on the stage being in a maze, under a misapprehension, "in a wood": if the spectators were too, the ironies would be lost. Wycherley specializes in these situations, as his title *Love in a Wood* hints. Short paraphrases of the plots of many Restoration comedies might suggest that the pleasures of the detective story are to be had from them: deep plots are laid by people intent on seeming different from what they really are, in order to get the girl or the inheritance or cuckold someone who deserves it. But these schemers either murmur "I'll answer as I should do" or "I cannot hold laughing" in asides to the audience, or confide their plans to friends dragged into the cast for this exclusive purpose; they take pains to see that the real state of affairs is made clear, and kept clear, to the meanest intelligence in the audience.[37] The pleasures of challenge and surprise are sacrificed to those of dramatic irony, whereby the audience savours the obtuseness of the cullies and bubbles on the stage. Like Oedipus, City husbands and fathers work out their own doom, bringing the dreaded event closer by every act of caution; and conversely, young heroes blunder their way into happiness, inviting disaster by fighting strangers in the dark, who turn out to be their best friends (as Aurelian and Hippolito also do, p. 55), making love to masked women who are really their sisters, and finally marrying the right woman by mistake. It is perhaps not true to say that all this could not be appreciated by an audience which was in the wood too, limited to the mistaken point of view of the protagonists; but it would be a completely different kind of appreciation. A more "modern" one, perhaps. Wycherley's plays would be impossible without the sardonic device of meanings in a character's lines of which the character is not himself aware, but the audience is. On a more general plane, the contrast between what is and what seems is such a basic and fruitful comic "theme" that it is difficult to write comedies in any period without using it. Congreve certainly wants to use it in *Incognita*. His characters are "in a wood," in a comic confusion which has received a great deal of care, and the reader must be out of the wood; must know how the knot will be unravelled, even as he sees it being tied.

At the same time, Congreve takes pains to make the obvious super-obvious, by such means as I exemplified at the beginning of this section. He describes the outcome in the very title of the book, and remarks every now and then that

---

[37] I think this is especially characteristic of the earlier Restoration comedy. Congreve usually follows the same pattern in his own plays; but, depending on how it is acted, the audience does not necessarily realize what Angelica in *Love for Love* is up to in the scene where she pretends to accept the addresses of Sir Sampson (V.i).

soon there is a big surprise coming, unless the reader has guessed it already, as he probably has, "if he be not the dullest reader in the world."

Thus, Congreve in *Incognita* mocks the conventions he himself is working within in a more radical way than the usual self-deprecating remarks about fantastic memories and such frills in the romances of the time; it is the most basic feature of all, the neatness itself, that is mocked, if, indeed, "mock" is the right word. Congreve emphasizes the most noticeable characteristics of his form; he exaggerates without distorting. In the comedies the references to stage conventions work because the audience is familiar with the conventions; and in the same way, Congreve's emphasis on the remarkable coincidences in *Incognita* work because the story is of a kind which the reader—even the modern reader—recognizes: the kind from which he expects a riot of remarkable circumstance. Such gentle satire is not at all characteristic of literary parody in the Restoration period, as I will try to show in the next chapter. *Incognita*'s sympathetic and merciful parody of a literary "world," rather than of any one genre, links it with the spirit of Restoration comedy.

V. Parody

i. Introduction

Incognita's "Preface to the Reader" is rather better known and more quoted than *Incognita* itself (cf. Appendix), especially Congreve's definition of the difference between novels and romances ("Romances give more of Wonder, Novels more Delight," etc.). This distinction is not, however, the only subject of the Preface; Congreve gives rather more space to his claim that he has imitated "Dramatick Writing." By dramatic writing he means comedy, since the novel is to the romance as comedy to tragedy—"with reverence be it spoken, and the Parallel kept at due distance." Partly, this imitation means simply that Congreve has adhered to the neo-classical dramatic "unities" of time, place and action: the reader is invited to consider

> whether every Obstacle does not in the progress of the Story act as subservient to that purpose, which at first it seems to oppose. In a Comedy this would be called the Unity of Action; here it may pretend to no more than an Unity of Contrivance. The scene is continued in Florence from the commencement of the Amour; and the time from first to last is but three days.

But that is not all, although Congreve with somewhat belated unassumingness leaves the reader to find the rest for himself:

> If there be any thing more in particular resembling the Copy which I imitate (as the Curious Reader will soon perceive) I leave it to show it self, being very well satisfy'd how much more proper it had been for him to have found out this himself, than for me to prepossess him with an Opinion of something extraordinary in an Essay began and finished in the idler hours of a fortnight's time.

Some critics have tried to show what exactly there is "more in particular resembling" the drama in *Incognita*, apart from the neatness of design resulting from the adherence to the unities. Thus Wilhelm Krohne thinks that *Incognita* has an easily perceived three-act structure with five scenes in each act,[1] while Günter Schopper prefers a five-act structure.[2] Besides, Schopper notes as resemblances to the drama that there is very little psychological motivation and description of inner states in the book, and that most of the

---

[1] Wilhelm Krohne, "Congreves Novelle *Incognita*," Diss. Münster 1924, pp. 50—53.
[2] Günter Schopper, *Aufbau und Sprache von Congreves "Incognita,"* Diss. Mainz 1967, p. 5.

information is conveyed to the reader in dialogue: thus, for instance, the enmity between the families of Aurelian and Juliana is not described to the reader directly, but he is allowed to overhear Leonora telling Hippolito about it (Schopper, pp. 12—13).

These resemblances to "drama" in general seem to me less significant (with the exception of the unity of action, of course, of which I have written extensively in Chapter IV) than the relation of *Incognita* to Restoration comedy in particular, which is surely the form Congreve himself was most likely to have had in mind when he wrote "the Copy which I imitate." The more general and superficial resemblances to "Dramatick Writing" in fact often seem more inept than anything else. Congreve seems to be trying to import certain features from the drama merely to show that he could, and to give the "Curious Reader" something to exercise his ingenuity in looking for. Thus the exposition in dialogue which Schopper writes about seems like pointless cleverness. The problem of exposition, that is, informing the audience of the state of affairs at the beginning of the play by the roundabout method of having the characters of the play inform each other of it, is usually very frankly faced in seventeenth-century drama. Beaumont and Fletcher especially are not interested in seamless, invisible exposition ("You are the brother to the king, my lord," a prince is helpfully told by an attendant at the opening of *The Maid's Tragedy*, I.l.3), and Congreve's "dramatic exposition" in *Incognita* shows the same fine disregard for the pifflingly "well made": "You know," says Leonora to Hippolito whom she mistakes for her Cousin Lorenzo, "the hatred Don Fabritio has born you ever since you had the fortune to kill his Kinsman in a Duel." Although this conversation, where Leonora goes so far as to refer to herself as "your Cousin Leonora," gives both the reader and Hippolito a perfectly clear picture of the relationships and enmities attendant on the duel in question, Congreve proceeds to make it redundant by explaining the situation all over again in one of his omniscient asides to the reader a few pages later, rightly remarking that the reader must, however, have apprehended it already "if he be not the dullest Reader in the World" (p. 48). Nor is there any attempt to keep to the point of view of Hippolito throughout the scene of his conversation with Leonora: Congreve has imported the difficulty without any of the advantages.

Another feature which seems like a borrowing from stage practice is the sexily informal dress worn by the heroines in the crucial scenes of the respective courtships: Incognita appears in the guise of a beautiful boy in the rescue scene (pp. 72—73), and Leonora's loveliness is enhanced by "an undress" when Hippolito sees her in the garden, "more Careless than usual in her Attire, which he thought added as much as was possible to the abundance of her Charms" (p. 79). Such scenes of suggestive undress are very common in the romances, but they provide exactly the thing which is noticeably lacking in *Incognita*: a concrete description of the charming effect. Sidney has some extremely erotic pictures of beauty in distress with very little clothes on, and the amorous novels of Congreve's own time do the same sort of thing, in if possible still more colourful terms:

> *Maria* had newly risen, and with her Night-gown only thrown loose about her, had look'd out of the Window, just as her Father and *Dangerfield* were approaching the Gate, at the same Instant she cast her Eyes upon *Dangerfield*, and he accidentally look'd up to the Window where she stood, their Surprise was mutual, but that of *Dangerfield* the greater; he saw such an amazing Sight of Beauty, as made him doubt the Reality of the Object, or distrust the Perfection of his Sight; he saw his dear Lady, who had so captivated him the preceeding Day, he saw her in all the heightning Circumstances of her Charms, he saw her in all her native Beauties, free from the Incumbrance of Dress, her Hair as black as Ebony hung flowing in careless Curls over her Shoulders, it hung link'd in amorous Twinings, as if in Love with its own Beauties; her Eyes not yet freed from the Dullness of the late Sleep, cast a languishing Pleasure in their Aspect, which heaviness of Sight added the greatest Beauties to those Suns, because under the Shade of such a Cloud, their Lustre cou'd only be view'd; the lambent Drowsiness that play'd upon her Face, seem'd like a thin Veil not to hide, but to heighten the Beauty which it cover'd; her Night-gown hanging loose, discover'd her charming Bosom, which cou'd bear no Name, but Transport, Wonder and Extasy, all which struck his Soul, as soon as the Object hit his Eye; her Breasts with an easy Heaving, show'd the Smoothness of her Soul and of her Skin; their Motions were so languishingly soft, that they cou'd not be said to rise and fall, but rather to swell up towards Love, the Heat of which seem'd to melt them down again; some scatter'd jetty Hairs, which hung confus'dly over her Breasts, made her Bosom show like *Venus* caught in *Vulcan's* Net, but 'twas the Spectator, not she, was captivated.

The classical reference at the end, and the "conceits" about clouds and suns, are hardly enough to soften the erotic impact of this breathless single sentence from Aphra Behn's *The Dumb Virgin*.[3] By comparison, the undress and the boy's clothes in *Incognita* read like mere stage directions. Of course such effects were common in Restoration comedy—especially the boy's clothes, showing the legs—and provided popular opportunities for the male part of the audience to admire an actress' figure.[4] Congreve's little essays into the suggestive really call out for an actual audience, or else an exceptionally imaginative reader: he does not mention whether Incognita's legs were in fact handsome or not. It remains true that "Jeremy Collier might have read the most liberal adventures of Aurelian without a blush."[5] I do not, of course, mean to imply that Congreve tried to be semi-pornographic and failed: that his

---

[3] In *Works*, V, 432–33.

[4] See John H. Wilson, "In Petticoat and Breeches," in *All the King's Ladies* (Chicago, 1958), pp. 67–86.

[5] H. F. B. Brett-Smith, ed., *Incognita*, pp. vii–viii.

aims were or ought to have been the same which Aphra Behn so triumphantly realized in the passage quoted above. He wished to be decorous: but, even so, his references to female charms are clearly more of the drama than the novel.

More generally, the situational humour of many scenes in *Incognita* seems to demand to be given "that life [...] which it has in the Action" (Preface, p. 33) in order to come across quite fully, as Palmer implies when he calls *Incognita* "a scenario."[6] Wilhelm Krohne among others[7] admires, for example, the sardonic comedy of Aurelian's headlong flight from an unrecognized lady visitor in his lodgings who is really his beloved Incognita, and of the immediately following scene where the two reverend fathers of Aurelian and Incognita also turn up in the ante-room, looking for Aurelian and running into the veiled Incognita. Krohne thinks this kind of thing shows that Congreve was already thinking in terms of stage comedy: "Es müsste auf der Bühne ein komischer Anblick sein, wenn Viterbo vor seiner eigenen Tochter höfliche Entschuldigungen stammelt."[8] Undeniably, it would have been comical on the stage, if cleverly produced, and it is fairly comical in the narration, too; but such situational ironies consistently demand a very concentrated and visually energetic reader.

These manifestations of dramatic influence in *Incognita* are clearly not exclusively fortunate, and on the whole trivial. A much more important justification for Congreve's prefatorial preoccupation with comedy is that *Incognita* shares the lightness of touch, the "perfectly humane" (Meredith's phrase) comic attitude of the best Restoration comedies.

The lightness of touch of Restoration comedy, the characteristic note of the best comedies of the period, is incisively defined by Kathleen M. Lynch. Following Palmer,[9] she sees the distinction between the Truewits and the Witwouds[10] as the basis of these comedies, and the fact that they are *both* to be laughed at as "the unfailing identification mark of all Restoration comedy," and as proof that the influence of Molière was only superficial:

The social posing of a Millamant [...] obviously produces a different sort of comic effect from the social posing of a Sir Fopling Flutter. Millamant represents good form, Sir Fopling bad form; her group can appropriately laugh at the follies of his, while the outsider can laugh, besides, at the affectations of hers. Here, surely, is a variety of

---

[6] John Palmer, *The Comedy of Manners* (London, 1913), p. 145.
[7] Cf. H. F. B. Brett-Smith, ed., *Incognita*, p. xii.
[8] Krohne, "Congreves Novelle *Incognita*," p. 67.
[9] *Comedy of Manners*.
[10] Made by Congreve in the preface to *The Way of the World*: "For this Play had been Acted two or three Days, before some of these hasty Judges cou'd find the leisure to distinguish betwixt the Character of a *Witwoud* and a *Truewit*" (*The Complete Plays of William Congreve*, ed. Herbert Davis, p. 390).

comic outlook possible only in the highly sophisticated society which this type of comedy represents. One may search in vain in Elizabethan drama and in the drama of Molière for a similar consistent contrast of comic standards. It is the unfailing identification mark of all Restoration comedy, and clearly serves to distinguish the type from all related forms.[11]

Palmer had seen this distinctive comic pattern as a new and independent creation of the Restoration period, an unconditioned reflexion of Restoration society; but Lynch goes one step further, and traces its growth out of the elaborate amatory ceremonial of *précieuse* gallantry introduced at the English court a generation earlier by Charles I's French queen Henrietta Maria. With the Civil War,

> the romantic splendors of Platonism were extinguished, not again to be restored. Yet Platonic formalities still survived in cavalier society, and under their moulding influence the new comedy developed. In the new comedy *précieuse* dialogue was still elaborated although it no longer had serious arguments to phrase. *Précieuse* gallantry was still gracefully enforced, but it now signified only a conventional habit of courtship. This now thoroughly conventionalized social mode was discovered to have manifestly comic aspects, both when awkwardly misinterpreted, and when completely fulfilled through personalities to which, however, it could not give complete expression. (p. 216)

This analysis is presumably the basis of Berkeley's formula that Restoration comedy is the inofficial view of the *précieuse* art of love—the "body" as against the "soul"—which I took advantage of in III:ii above. The characteristic relation between "body" and "soul" of Restoration comedy at its best, which Lynch maps with such precision, characterizes Congreve's *Incognita* too. Congreve surely owes to this special Restoration version of "Dramatick Writing" the perception that the fictional conventions available to him could have "manifestly comic aspects," not only when hilariously misinterpreted in burlesque writing, but also when completely fulfilled in a form which at the same time expressed an awareness of their limitations. In the preceding chapters, I tried to show how *Incognita* embodies this perception in its very structure, as well as in all the little mini-parodies of Congreve's fashionably "self-conscious" style. *Incognita* is a sympathetic, cherishing parody, very different from the usual temper of literary parody in the Restoration period.

ii. Restoration Parody

The contemporary tradition of parody available to Congreve was certainly of a thumpingly unsympathetic character, to put it no more strongly. Congreve's sympathetic mockery seems out of place in its contemporary setting. Such

---

[11] Kathleen M. Lynch, *The Social Mode of Restoration Comedy* (New York, 1926), p. 7.

mockery had only, barely, been developed (principally by Etherege) for the handling of characters in the comedies: Congreve applies it to literary forms, the parody of which was otherwise a field of robustness, of the sledgehammer rather than the rapier. It is perhaps significant that *The Rehearsal*, which I will have occasion to compare with *Incognita* in this respect, is very much more particular and topical than *Incognita*: it was written to make fun of Dryden— "Bayes"— rather than of the heroic play in general, and it mocks Dryden's personal mannerisms almost as much as his plays. There is personal animus, as well as good humour, in it, and this no doubt makes the method of incongruity and travesty the most natural one. The most popular type of literary parody in the Restoration period, the burlesque of classical authors, which was patterned on Scarron's *Virgile travesti* (1648), [12] displays the same animus. The authors (Charles Cotton is the best known of them) took a classical story and retold it in a farcical way, with obscene mishaps, supposedly comic similes, and highly coloured, highly contemporary and topical dialogue. It is essentially a schoolboy joke: these burlesques were immensely popular, surely because the readers had themselves been literally whipped through Virgil at school. With such a background, it did not much matter that Scarron's often witty travesty was coarsened beyond recognition in the imitation: the revenge on the childhood bogey was sweet anyway, perhaps sweeter the more crudely he was treated. It is understandable that the endless repetitions of the same incongruities and anachronisms, now infinitely boring, should have been endlessly enjoyable to many contemporary readers.

The word "burlesque" has a different, less specific, meaning now, but it retains its back-slapping, outrageous, sub-cultural connotations. The seventeenth-century burlesque was not considered respectable, not "literature" at all: it was despised by readers of any cultural pretensions (though they may have read it in secret), as well as by later literary historians.[13] In France, Boileau discredited not only its crudest exponents but the method itself in his *L'Art poétique* (1674).[14] In *Le Lutrin* (also 1674), he himself gave a practical example of the other, remaining logical way of bringing high and low into comic collision: namely, clothing a slight or "low" subject in full epic machinery and dignity of style. In the preface to the first edition he called it "a new burlesque":

C'est un Burlesque nouveau, dont je me suis avisé en nostre Langue. Car au lieu que dans l'autre Burlesque Didon et Enée parloient comme des Harangeres et des Crocheteurs; dans celui-ci une Horlogere et un Horloger parlent comme Didon et Enée.[15]

---

[12] See Sturgis E. Leavitt, "Paul Scarron and English Travesty," *SP*, 16 (1919), 108–20.
[13] Ibid.
[14] Chant I, 79–97; *Œuvres complètes*, ed. Charles-H. Boudhors, I (Paris, 1939), 83–84.
[15] *Œuvres complètes*, I, 169.

Later (in 1711, according to the *OED*) this new burlesque was distinguished from its obverse the old one by the name of mock-heroic. It turned out to be capable of developments far more subtle than the principle of simple incongruity: its history is adorned by such names as Garth, Dryden and Pope.[16] In fact, it is not literary parody at all, but is used for the mockery and/or cherishing of larger matters (at least, other matters) than the literary form. The epic form is not parodied, or probed, or questioned in *McFlecknoe* and *The Rape of the Lock*: it is the vehicle of Dryden's political satire, and of Pope's image of society. These works are consequently not comparable in this respect with *Incognita*. Congreve is *interested* in the form, in testing it and playing with it, just as he was later to use the comedy to test and play with ideas about sexual relationships and marriage. He is rather, therefore, to be compared with Buckingham and Cotton: but his attitude is radically different from theirs. It is surely Congreve's receptivity to the spirit of Restoration comedy, which he was afterwards to embody so perfectly in his own comedies, that explains and defines his special position in Restoration parody. His method is not that of travesty.

iii. Literary Clichés

Incognita embodies an awareness of the comic possibilities of its own conventions in its very structure, as I argued above; but in the experience of reading the book, the impression of serious mockery, of parody that does not distort, is not derived from this elevated plane alone. It is solidified on almost every page by Congreve's distancing, ironic treatment of details in the literary tradition that is his element in *Incognita*. It is impossible to illustrate this with more than a few characteristic examples, which I will try to compare with examples of more "normal" seventeenth-century parody.

The tournament is perhaps the most characteristic of all. Nothing could be more literary than Congreve's inclusion of that overworked romance episode: a jousting to celebrate a royal, or as in this case a ducal, wedding. Congreve is really at least a hundred years too late to do that sort of thing seriously. Writers with realistic pretensions had been making fun of the romancers' fondness for tournaments for the last century, often by insincerely apologizing for the inability of their own plain blunt work to rise to such heights. In the afterword to *Iphigene* (1625), Camus had complained that the narrative of "les

---

[16] See the introduction to *The Rape of the Lock*, in *The Twickenham Edition of the Poems of Alexander Pope*, II, ed. Geoffrey Tillotson (1940; rev. ed. London, 1954), 83—126.

romanciers ordinaires" delayed itself ever and again to describe tourneys, and runnings at the ring (which is also the first part of Congreve's tournament, although he does not exactly describe it) and carousels, organized for some princely wedding, "et la moindre part de leur hyménée, ce sont les mariez."[17] Congreve works on a much smaller scale than these ordinary romancers: he gives us as it were a miniature of the full-dress romance jousting, with its massive descriptions of the arms, mottoes and devices of the combatants, and its monotonous lists of combats, which all seem very similar to the non-aficionado. But he includes all the essentials, giving them half a sentence each instead of half a chapter or fytte. The colours and devices, the description of which had reached a logical climax in the grotesquely allegorical trappings worn in *The Unfortunate Traveller*,[18] are here rendered with suitable conciseness:

Hippolito wore upon his Helm a large Plume of Crimson Feathers, in the midst of which was artificially placed Leonora's Handkerchief. His Armour was gilt, and enammell'd with Green and Crimson. Aurelian was not so happy as to wear any token to recommend him to the notice of his Mistress, so had only a Plume of Sky-colour and White Feathers, suitable to his Armour, which was silver enammelled with Azure. (pp. 62–63)

Such details are so definitely of the romance that even Boyle in *Parthenissa* (1654–76) had made his avoidance of them a claim to realism, to truthfulness (see II:ii above): "But not to dress a true story in cloaths of a Romance, I will pass by the descriptions of our Arms, Devices, Motto's, and all things of so low a nature..."

But descriptions of tournaments were not simply old-fashioned in 1692: they are the sort of setpiece which has always, at any time, had a period flavour. It had always been artificial and literary. The activity itself, not only the conventional description of it, is stylized and reduced to a formula. The tournament is a patterned, idealized, manageable version of the chaos of actual battle, perhaps via the traditional literary conception of battle as a collection of single combats: nature imitating art.[19]

Of course this idealized version may equally well be regarded as a debased,

---

[17] Quoted by Magendie (p. 141), who traces the literary jousting to the battle scenes in the *Aeneid*, via the *Gerusalemme Liberata*.

[18] Thomas Nashe, *The Vnfortvnate Traveller: or The Life of Jacke Wilton*, ed. H. F. B. Brett-Smith, The Percy Reprints, No. 1 (Oxford, 1927), pp. 67–75. This tournament takes place in Florence too, like the very different one in *Incognita*.

[19] Charles Muscatine makes this point in *Chaucer and the French Tradition*: "Poetically, the settings of *Guillaume de Dole* or *L'Escoufle* are no more realistic than our own reports of opening nights at the opera. French courtly society at its most magnificent, with its tournaments and feasts and hunts, if not partly imitating romance, certainly approached the ideality of it" (p. 15).

unreal pretence, lacking the substance of that which is imitated. Walter R. Davis suggests that Sidney uses it in this way in the *Arcadia*, which contains both tournaments and real battles. Thus the gallantry and compliments of the cowardly knight Phalantus are, writes Davis, "to Argalus' and Amphialus' love as his formal tournaments are to their real experience of battle."[20] Phalantus has no very good reason for all his jousting: he travels from country to country with his lady Artesia holding tournaments to maintain the supremacy of her beauty against all comers, merely because she has trapped him into a pledge to do it. Yet surely this is nature itself compared to the purpose of the tournament in *Incognita*, where the beauty of the noble bride is a priori "above the insolence of competition," regardless not only of her face (the actual looks of Artesia have nothing to do with the whole thing, either), but of any fighting spirit in the challengers, too: nobody is allowed to fight. In one way, this is an advance in realism: Congreve is getting one of the traditional high spots of the romance into his story without absolutely renouncing probability. In the vaguely but unmistakably modern Florence of *Incognita* something not too unlike—if not too like, either—a jousting of this purely honorary kind might actually have taken place, at least within a century or two of 1692.[21] Only three years before that date, the coronation of William and Mary in London had contained a notable parallel to Congreve's honorary challenge "only designed for show and form" (p. 63) on behalf of Donna Catharina.[22] The challenge of the King's Champion was one of the traditional ceremonies attendant on the coronation.[23] A "Herald with a loud Voice" proclaimed that if anybody should deny the title of William and Mary,

> here is his CHAMPION, who saith that he lieth, and is a false Traitor, being ready in Person to Combat with him; and in this Quarrel will adventure his Life against him, on what Day soever he shall be appointed.[24]

The challenge being proclaimed, the champion threw down his gauntlet and allowed it to lie "some small time"; then it was picked up and returned by a herald. By imitating this kind of stylized but actual and contemporary event (whether or not he had the coronation specifically in mind), Congreve can

---

[20] Walter R. Davis, "A Map of Arcadia: Sidney's Romance in Its Tradition," in *Sidney's Arcadia*, Yale Studies in English, No. 158 (New Haven, 1965), p. 116.

[21] See "Torneo," *Encyclopedia Italiana*.

[22] Maximillian E. Novak suggests in "Congreve's *Incognita* and the Art of the Novella" that the three days' festivities in *Incognita* were inspired by the carnival atmosphere surrounding the recent coronation (p. 331).

[23] See Macaulay, *History of England*, Vol. I—IV of *Works* (London, 1873), II, 490.

[24] *An Account of the Ceremonies Observed at the Coronation of the Kings and Queens of England* (London, 1727), p. 25; cf. also the *London Gazette*, No. 2444, April 11 to April 15, 1689.

have his tournament, without having to resort to the medieval fantasy of Nashe's extravagant variations on the old theme. The episode shows, then, a concern for *vraisemblance* in a very technical sense, but of course it also represents an extreme of abstraction and stylization: it presents as it were only the first term of Sidney's contrast between artificial and real. Davis describes this contrast:

> The tournament itself serves as a ceremonial establishment of the theme of love in *Arcadia*, and emhasizes the difference between the loves we have seen in the past and those of our two heroes. The first seven combats are colourless ceremonial affairs in which Phalantus easily defeats several mere courtly servants while the lover Pyrocles chafes under the restraint of his disguise. Upon this rather meaningless order of events there suddenly bursts genuine feeling: from opposite ends of the field ride the Black Knight (Musidorus) and the Ill Appointed Knight (Pyrocles) [. . .]. The old formal seeming is defeated by a new active love, the farce ends.[25]

In *Incognita*, the sudden burst, the gesture towards a defeat of the formal seeming, is so abortive that it only reinforces the artificial game: we are never brought out of it at all. Aurelian and Hippolito make the mistake of taking up the challenge, of taking the formal seeming for reality. They see a picture of a lady, and think "themselves obliged, especially in the presence of their Mistresses, to vindicate their Beauty" (p. 63), as Congreve puts it, making it clear from the outset that even the taking up of the challenge by the heroes has a good dose of "show and form" in it. Nevertheless, in the frame in which it occurs, it is *more* real than the rest, more real than is expected or polite inside the game. We know, after all, that Aurelian and Hippolito both do think their respective loves the most beautiful lady in the world, even though they are more concerned with politeness and *machismo* at the moment (Congreve does not mention whether the picture they see is handsome or not; who is actually the prettiest lady does not interest him at all). Fortunately for the integrity of the game, their faux pas of starting for Donna Catharina's champion is interrupted, and they are told

> that it was the Picture of Donna Catharina, and a particular Honour done to her by his Highness's Commands, and not to be disputed. Upon this they would have returned to their Post, much concerned for their mistake; . . . (pp. 63–64)

In these heroes there is no threat to the sublimely "meaningless order of events." With incomparable good breeding, they send a "Complement" to the bride,

> wherein, having first begg'd her pardon for not knowing her Picture, they gave her to understand, that now they were not about to dispute her undoubted right to the

---

[25] "A Map of Arcadia: Sidney's Romance in Its Tradition," p. 116.

Crown of Beauty, but the honour of being her Champions was the Prize they fought for, which they thought themselves as able to maintain as any other Pretenders.

Begging her pardon for not knowing her picture is not really very flattering to the lady, if you take it apart.

The tournament is the most well-worn and tradition-encrusted of all the elements Congreve plays with in *Incognita*, and he puts it to a highly characteristic use, making it more stylized even than he received it, stressing its artificiality by introducing a pseudo-escape, a quickly baffled mock breakout from the narrowly defined game which he plays so gracefully. It is instructive to compare this distancing extra dimension with the way Nashe handles the same theme in outrageous all-out parody. Congreve's tournament is to Nashe's burlesque version in *The Unfortunate Traveller* as Mirabell is to Witwoud in *The Way of the World*, or as Etherege's Dorimant to Sir Fopling Flutter. Congreve plays with literary clichés in *Incognita* in the same spirit in which he and Etherege handle human individuals in their plays. The model for Congreve's parody is that contemporary comedy which "owes its distinctive comic harmony to the genial and sympathetic laughter which its finer characters inspire" (Lynch, p. 8), rather than any work of parody available to him; although he directs the "genial and sympathetic laughter" of the reader towards fine literary clichés instead of fine characters.

If Congreve's tournament is the most perfect embodiment of the spirit of humane parody which informs *Incognita*, the "God-huffing" of Aurelian is another illustrative manifestation of it. The conflict between love and duty draws from him the following lament:

"Oh ye unequal powers, why do ye urge us to desire what ye doom us to forbear; give us a Will to chuse, then curb us with a Duty to restrain that Choice! Cruel Father, Will nothing else suffice! Am I to be the Sacrifice to expiate your Offences past; past ere I was born? Were I to lose my Life, I'd gladly Seal your Reconcilement with my Blood. But Oh my Soul is free, you have no Title to my Immortal Being, that has Existence independent of your Power; and must I lose my Love, the Extract of that Being, the Joy, Light, Life, and Darling of my Soul? No, I'll own my Flame, and plead my Title too. —But hold, wretched Aurelian, hold, whither does thy Passion hurry thee? Alas! The cruel fair Incognita Loves thee not! She knows not of thy Love! If she did, what Merit hast thou to pretend?—Only Love.—Excess of Love. And all the World has that. All that have seen her. Yet I had only seen her once, and in that once I lov'd above the World; nay, lov'd beyond my self, such vigorous Flame, so strong, so quick she darted at my Breast; it must rebound, and by Reflection, warm her self. Ah! welcome Thought, lovely deluding Fancy, hang still upon my Soul, let me but think, that once she Loves and perish my Despair." (pp. 67—68)

Aurelian quickly reasons himself out of the conflict, we see, and into a decision on love's side. Nevertheless, this is a recognizable version of the favourite theme of the Spanish and Spain-influenced novels of the seventeenth century: the conflict between love and duty. The phrase had a narrow and specific application: "duty" does not mean the general demands of ethics and morality, but the obligation to obey, to be "dutiful" to, parents and guardians, preferably unreasonable and crotchety ones so as to make the conflict more outré. It is only one aspect of the theme of morality interfering with desire, and there are other special phrases for other aspects of the nagging *précieuse* fascination with the ramifications of this problem. "The conflict between love and friendship" had a vogue among the *précieux* groups in England,[26] and can be studied as late as in the serious action of Etherege's *Love in a Tub* (1664). And of course "the conflict between love and honour"—where "honour" stands for military glory, often with some "duty" in the above sense thrown in—was the dominant theme of the heroic play, which flourished in the first two decades of the Restoration. The agonized struggle between the two opposing principles of this "conflict" is rendered with unforgettable concreteness in *The Rehearsal*, when Prince Volscius debates with himself whether to put his boots on and go to war, or keep them off and stay at home with his beloved:

> *Bayes.* Here, now, Mr. *Johnson,* you shall see a combat betwixt Love and Honour. An Ancient Author has made a whole Play on't; but I have dispatch'd it all in this Scene.
>
> Volscius *sits down to pull on his Boots:* Bayes *Stands by and over acts the Part as he speaks it.*
>
> > *Volscius.* How has my Passion Made me *Cupid*'s scoff!
> > This hasty Boot is on, the other off,
> > And sullen lies, with amorous design
> > To quit loud fame, and make that Beauty mine.
> > [. . .]
> > Shall I to Honour or to Love give way?
> > Go on, cries Honour; tender Love saies, nay:
> > Honour, aloud, commands, pluck both Boots on;
> > But softer Love does whisper put on none.
> > What shall I do? what conduct shall I find
> > To lead me through this twy-light of my mind?
> > For as bright Day with black approach of Night
> > Contending, makes a doubtful puzling light;
> > So does my Honour and my Love together
> > Puzzle me so, I can resolve for neither.
> > [*Goes out hopping with one Boot on, and the other off.*[27]

Although the seventeenth-century "conflict" literature rises to the tragic in a few cases, its remorseless and humourless elaborations in the hands of its less

---

[26] As represented by Lodowick Carlell and others; see Lynch, *The Social Mode of Restoration Comedy*, p. 63.

[27] George Villiers, Duke of Buckingham, *The Rehearsal*, ed. Montague Summers (Stratford-upon-Avon, 1914), pp. 41–42.

gifted enthusiasts surely calls out for some such parody as this memorable externalization of the conflict in the hero's breast in the emblematic figure of the boots. I bring in Buckingham's parody here as a contrast to Congreve's: it is "normal" or "major" seventeenth-century parody, radically burlesque. In Congreve's delicately balanced parody, the warring principles are reconciled by a stroke of good fortune—Aurelian's beloved turns out to be identical with the prudent choice of his father—which was of course no novelty, whatever the second term of the "conflict." While a real conflict is tragic, one that can be resolved so facilely is either trivial or comic. In the peculiar tragi-comic world of the heroic play, potential tragedy is degraded by the deadly idea of poetic justice: "The hero who renounced love in order to meet the demands of honour, like Dryden's Almanzor, normally contrived to enjoy both; the hero who yielded to love, like Otway's Jaffeir or Dryden's Montezuma, paid for it dearly."[28] Congreve's providence in *Incognita* displays the Restoration virtue of complaisance rather than justice: it is by choosing love that Aurelian contrives to enjoy both. His qualms are serious enough in the passage I have just quoted, however, even if by heroic standards he gets over them rather quickly. But the passage goes on:

Here a suddain stop gave a Period also to Hippolito's Expectation, and he hoped now that his Friend had given his Passion so free a vent, he might recollect and bethink himself of what was convenient to be done; but Aurelian, as if he had mustered up all his Spirits purely to acquit himself of that passionate Harangue, stood mute and insensible like an Alarum Clock, that had spent all its force in one violent Emotion. (p. 68)

The seventeenth-century heroic hero in the grip of a conflict never did bethink himself of what was convenient to be done (the heroes of the comedies were a little more active); and Aurelian is being truly heroic here. Whether the second term of the conflict was duty, friendship or honour, its petrifying effect on the hero was the same: it produced talk, not action. This tendency is well-known and conspicuous in the case of the heroic play, but it is equally characteristic of the romances. The heroic or romantic hero of the seventeenth century who found himself in a difficult situation that could not be handled by simply fighting did not usually descend to any other practical measures; he made a speech on the cruelty of fate. To try to think of something to do was apparently considered, if not exactly contemptible, yet certainly more fitting for characters on a slightly lower plane of existence than the hero, for example his friend and confidant. In Congreve's own tragedy *The Mourning Bride* (1697) this

---

[28] Clifford Leech, "Restoration Tragedy: A Reconsideration," *Durham University Journal*, 11 (1950), rpt. in *Restoration Drama: Modern Essays in Criticism*, ed. John Loftis (New York, 1966), p. 147.

division of labour between hero and friend is exhibited so pointedly in one passage as to border on the mock-heroic. The rightful heir Prince Alphonso (under the alias of Osmyn) languishes in despair in prison, but revives when his friend Heli (also called Antonio) tells him that the people are ripe for mutiny and in need of a leader:

> *Osmyn.* By Heav'n thou'st rous'd me from my Lethargy.
> The Spirit which was deaf to my own Wrongs,
> Deaf to revenge, and the loud Crys of my
> Dead Father's Blood; Nay, which refus'd to hear
> The Piercing Sighs, and Murmurs of my Love
> Yet unenjoy'd; what not *Almeria* could
> Revive, or raise, my Peoples Voice has wak'ned
> O my *Antonio*, I am all on Fire,
> My Soul is up in Arms, ready to charge
> And bear amidst the Foe, with conqu'ring Troops.
> I hear 'em call to lead 'em on to Liberty,
> To Victory; their Shouts and Clamours rend
> My Ears, and reach the Heav'ns; where is the King?
> Where is *Alphonso*? ha! where? where indeed?
> O I could tear and burst the Strings of Life,
> To break these Chains. Off, off, ye Stains of Royalty.
> Off Slavery. O curse! that I alone
> Can beat and flutter in my Cage, when I
> Would soar, and stoop at Victory beneath.
>
> *Heli.* Our Posture of Affairs and scanty Time,
> My Lord, require you should compose your self,
> And think on what we may reduce to Practise.
>   (III.i.73—94)

This splendid comment of Heli-Antonio's on the ineffectual heroic attitude is all the better for the way Alphonso starts his harangue *as if* he were going to do something practical ("By Heav'n thou'st rous'd me from my Lethargy"[29]), and then runs down into the usual helpless "curse," disappointing as Aurelian does his friend's hope that he will produce a concrete plan of action. Of course the comments is suitably more oblique in the tragedy: it does not cross the line into the mock-heroic, as it does in *Incognita*. Not only does Congreve place Aurelian's histrionic exclamation just where some brisk action is particularly called for, but he adds the wonderfully expressive image of the heroic hero as an emotional alarm-clock. Compared to burlesque parody, as exemplified by *The Rehearsal*, *Incognita*'s version is oblique—or "perfectly humane"—too, but it is also perfectly clear and pointed.

[29] Congreve likes this phrase in this connection; he has already used it in *Incognita*, immediately after the passage where Aurelian runs down like an alarm-clock: "Hippolito shook him by the Arm to rouze him from his Lethargy."

Equally graceful is the comic resolution of the threatening *précieuse* conflict between love and friendship[30] which Leonora finds herself faced with. This conflict—sometimes in the more general form of a dilemma where the hero/heroine had to choose between renouncing his/her love and injuring a third person, whether a friend or not—was the one that lent itself most readily to being honed fine into an extravagant scrupulousness, and in that form it passed to the sentimental heroes and heroines in the weeping comedy of Steele and his contemporaries.[31] As in the case of "love and honour," *The Rehearsal* provides a version which speaks volumes:

> 3 *Player. (Reads. The Argument of the Fifth Act.) Cloris* at length, being sensible of Prince *Pretty-man's* passion, consents to marry him; but, just as they are going to Church, Prince *Pretty-man* meeting, by chance, with old *Joan* the Chandlers widdow, and remembring it was she first brought him acquainted with *Cloris*: out of a high point of honour, brake off his match with *Cloris*, and marries old *Joan*.
>
> (p. 70)

This radical burlesque can surely be appreciated by any age. Congreve's version, again, is more subtle and also more surprising. His Leonora makes a brief appearance in the role of scrupulous heroine when she receives a written declaration of love from the false Aurelian, actually Hippolito, who she thinks is engaged to her friend Juliana; but she manages to conquer the unwelcome qualm, indeed to triumph over it:

> ... how could she consent to Marry a Man already Destined for another Woman? nay, a Woman that was her Friend, whose Marrying with him was to compleat the happy Reconciliation of Two Noble Families, and which might prevent the Effusion of much Blood likely to be shed in that Quarrel: Besides, she should incurr share of the Guilt, which he would draw upon him by Disobedience to his Father, whom she was sure would not be consenting to it.
>
> 'Tis strange now, but all Accounts agree, that just here Leonora, who had run like a violent Stream against Aurelian hitherto, now retorted with as much precipitation in his Favour. I could never get any Body to give me a satisfactory reason, for her suddain and dextrous Change of Opinion just at that stop, which made me conclude she could not help it; and that Nature boil'd over in her at that time when it had so fair an Opportunity to show it self: For Leonora it seems was a Woman Beautiful, and otherwise of an excellent Disposition; but in the Bottom a very Woman. This last Objection, this

---

[30] According to S. L. Wolff (*The Greek Romances*, pp. 248—55), this useful old standby comes from the Greek romances. Wolff posits a lost Byzantine novel as the origin of the various versions of the medieval "Legend of Two Friends," of which Boccaccio's "Tito and Gisippo" (*Decamerone* X:8) and Lyly's *Euphues* (which uses Boccaccio's story as a source, but lets love win instead of friendship, in the same situation) are offshoots. The lost novel may conceivably be that which Goldsmith professes to have translated in *Septimus and Alcander* (*The Bee*, No. 1, 1759), assuming that it is true that Goldsmith used a "Byzantine Historian," as he claimed.

[31] See David S. Berkeley, *The Précieuse, or Distressed Heroine, of Restoration Comedy*, Oklahoma State University Publications, 56, No. 19 (Stillwater, Oklahoma, 1959).

Opportunity of perswading a Man to Disobedience, determined the Matter in Favour of Aurelian, more than all his Excellencies and Qualifications, take him as Aurelian, or Hippolito, or both together. (pp. 60—61)

Thus the honourable hesitation becomes an argument *for* love: love and duty reconciled indeed.

It is not so much Leonora we are being invited to laugh at here (although there is that too), as the whole rich complex of literary associations adhering to her situation, her conflict. Congreve's little ironies at the expense of his characters (cf. III:iv above) are far too slight and unspecific to be considered even an early sketch for the rich comic characterization of his plays; in fact, in the context of his plays, it is misleading to use the term "characters" with reference to *Incognita* at all. In *Incognita* it is the literary clichés, not the people, that get the real characterization. On the whole, the dissimilarities between *Incognita* and the comedies, in tone, spirit and technique, are more striking than the resemblances.[32] *Incognita* is altogether more "literary" than Congreve's plays; it is not *like* them, but it may nevertheless in important ways be regarded as a necessary prologue to them.

---

[32] Many critics consider *Incognita* far more similar to Restoration comedy than I do, although they compare it rather with the earlier comedy than with Congreve's own plays: see for example Montague Summers, Intr. pp. 4—5; and Brett-Smith, Intr. pp. xi—xii.

VI. *Incognita* and the Comedies

I mentioned the ambiguous, double character of the episode of the tournament above (p. 83): as a well-worn romantic setpiece it contributes to the literary and recognizable feeling of *Incognita*, while at the same time it is a credible enough account of the kind of purely honorary event which really took place occasionally in the seventeenth century. The names of the four main characters—Aurelian, Hippolito, Juliana, Leonora—share this characteristically reversible quality. They strike the reader as being out of the same box as Chloe and Belinda, and the last three are in fact common in romances; but at the same time they are perfectly fitted to contemporary actual Italians and Spaniards (Hippolito is a native of Spain: he also has a surname and a title, Don Hippolito di Savolina, as is common in the seventeenth-century realistic Spanish novel, while the others have just first names, in the accepted romantic manner[1]).

It seems unlikely that Congreve consciously wanted exactly this hovering status for his proper names,[2] but it is there all the same: they "seem" literary, but "are" ordinary and contemporary, though of course foreign. The effect of literary-sounding proper names is not simple in itself, either. Mish points out that the endemic classicized names in Aphra Behn's novels, "Bellamora" and such, "are part of the effort to establish belief, since they are used so ostentatiously to conceal real names."[3] When we read that "Bellamora came to town from *Hampshire*"[4] (that is, from the most countrified and bumpkinly shire of all, in the estimation of the fashionable town writers, and the least likely to breed romance heroines), the reader's association is surely to the way such classicized names were used in lampoons and satires. Aphra Behn's Bellamora, then, is a roundabout but effective way of establishing belief, proclaiming not merely that this is life itself, but better still, "this is a *roman à clef*": not only did it all happen, but it was so sensational that the real names must be suppressed in the telling.

[1] "The primarily literary and conventional orientation of these proper names [before Defoe] was further attested by the fact that there was usually only one of them—Mr Badman or Euphues; unlike people in ordinary life, the characters of fiction did not have both given name and surname" (Ian Watt, *The Rise of the Novel*, p. 20).
[2] Montague Summers points out that they were partly lifted from Dryden's *Love in a Nunnery* (*The Complete Works of William Congreve*, 1924, rpt. New York, 1964, I, 4.).
[3] Mish, "English Short Fiction," p. 301, n. 126.
[4] The opening words of *The Adventure of the Black Lady*; *Works*, V, 3.

It is perhaps not surprising that the romantic-sounding proper names in *Incognita* should have inspired "Charles Wilson"—probably a pseudonym—to impute a spicy contemporary background to Congreve's novel, too. This he did in the *Memoir* of Congreve which was issued in 1730 by the irrepressible Curll:

Tho' the Scene of the foregoing Novel be laid in *Italy*, every Incident was transacted in *England*. But as some of the Persons are dead, and others living, yet 'till they are all gather'd to their Fathers, I dare not presume to decypher any one Character, especially since some Folks, much more grand in their Talk than their Power, threaten to prosecute us *to the Extent of their Fortunes, and the Hazard of our own Lives.*[5]

A more transparent publicity trick it would be difficult to conceive. The fictional quality of Congreve's story is emphasized throughout, as I have tried to show: the fictional quality is the heart of the book, since *Incognita* is a parody not only incidentally, like for instance the *Roman comique*, but essentially and on every level.

It is a natural development for a bookish young man to begin in this way: to approach the problems of life first via literature, by examining the ideas offered by literature, and to move towards the realistic and contemporary more as one's own experience broadens. It is perhaps a kind of cheating to read *Incognita* in the light of Congreve's plays: but it is, after all, interesting. He wrote *Incognita* as a very young man (even if he was not only seventeen, as the *Biographia Britannica* has it; see Introduction above), and his ideas about human and particularly sexual relationships are very tentative there; nevertheless, although the patterns of love and marriage which he plays with in *Incognita* are taken from literature, it is their relevance to life that interests him. This is not perhaps absolutely clear in *Incognita* itself, but becomes abundantly so in his later writings. *Incognita* traces the first steps in Congreve's search for a liveable, practical version of "the good life." He recognized that this had to be achieved by a combination of hard endeavour and luck, and that its attainment involved money, leisure, delicate emotional intelligence and practical prudence. The easy fortuitous but providential patterning of the romances and the Beaumont and Fletcher plays is inadequate, since men and women must work out their own salvations, while the *précieux* quandaries are too rarefied to have relevance to flesh and blood; yet in so far as they embody a human yearning for delicate beauty in emotional and above all sexual relationships, they are valuable. In consequence, all these things are subjected to a kind of cherishing ridicule in *Incognita*.

---

[5] Charles Wilson, *Memoirs of the Life, Writings, and Amours of William Congreve Esq.* (London, 1730), p. 125.

Bonamy Dobrée has suggested that Congreve in his comedies "had rather more to say than the mode he chose for speech would allow him; and one may suspect that it was the realization of this, combined with the failure of *The Way of the World*, that made him abandon the stage at the age of thirty."[6] This may be so, although *The Way of the World* seems to me a perfect expression of what Congreve wanted to say; but the statement may, in any case, be applied with far greater certainty to Congreve's abandonment of prose fiction after *Incognita*. In a sense, as I hope I have managed to convey in this thesis, the dissatisfaction with the medium is the subject of *Incognita*. The romance, being out-moded and out-of-touch, offered Congreve no further way of developing his interest in the emotional quality of life; while the trend towards "realistic" fiction was not only inadequately selective, but it relied too much on incident, whereas Congreve was really interested in attitude.

This becomes particularly clear in *The Double-Dealer*, with its too-visible seam between, on the one hand, the complicated plot of Maskwell's machinations, and on the other, the "problem play" within the play, which is concerned with the relationship between Mellefont and Cynthia. She loves him, but has doubts about marrying him, because of the painful spectacle of two very foolish, long-established marriages: the vulgar "fondness" of Lord and Lady Froth, and the tyranny of Lady Plyant over her uxorious Sir Paul. Mellefont argues that these marriages are deplorable simply because the four people concerned are foolish in themselves, but she is not sure:

Nay, I have known Two Wits meet, and by the opposition of their Wits, render themselves as ridiculous as Fools. 'Tis an odd Game we're going to Play at: What think you of drawing Stakes, and giving over in time?
(II.i.155—58)

The delicious comedy of the scenes where the Froths and Plyants bill and coo, and the full-length portraits of Lady Froth and Lady Plyant with their various vanities, are the nub of the play; not Maskwell and Lady Touchwood. And these scenes hardly bring the plot—the "plotty" plot—forward at all. To emphasize the rift further, Mellefont and Cynthia never seem really worried about the external, plot-induced obstacles to their marriage: particularly Cynthia obviously assumes that all that is not to be taken seriously, the only real problem to her is whether they *should* marry. The possible disinheritances and refusals of consent by guardians do not alarm her (and if she took her father's refusal of consent seriously, it ought to alarm her, since she is too dutiful a daughter to marry without it), but the Froths and their displays of silliness do. In his plays, Congreve could use dialogue to bring out the

---

[6] Bonamy Dobrée, "Congreve," in *Restoration Comedy* (Oxford, 1924), pp. 121—50, rpt. in *Restoration Drama: Modern Essays in Criticism*, ed. John Loftis (New York, 1966), p. 98.

attitudes of characters in relatively "realistic" relationships, even though convention demanded that he should also provide plenty of incident and external "obstacles" (in time, as we see in *The Way of the World*, he learned to integrate the two rather better); but in prose fiction incident was all, and to relieve it with longish stretches of dialogue, as Congreve does in *Incognita*, was not really much of a solution.

The method of Congreve's plays is foreshadowed in *Incognita*. In both, it is a question of making a work of art out of the material at hand, of working within a pattern: and in order to do this, the available pattern must first be mapped and tested, with all possible delicacy and penetration. In *Incognita*, it is mainly literature that is so tested; in the plays it is life itself.

To analyse the whole extremely complicated and subtle mapping of life in Congreve's comedies is probably impossible, and would in any case take up far too much space: I can only try to make my generalities a little more solid by a simple example.

In all his plays, Congreve brings in a pair of contrasting attitudes. In *The Old Batchelour*, it is two opposed ways of carrying on a courtship: Vainlove loves the pleasures of the chase, of pursuing an elusive mistress, but abhors compliance and "fondness," and consequently he finds an affair stale as soon as the lady grows kind, and fobs her off on Bellmour, who is only too delighted to take over, since he loves consummation better than preliminaries. In *The Double-Dealer*, it is contrasting ways of conducting a marriage, embodied in the Froths and the Plyants, whose humours I described above. In *Love for Love*, it is contrasting ways of taking care of the ladies' reputations in affairs with married women: Scandal versus Tattle. Tattle sets up for discretion and secrecy—"trusty Mr. Tattle"—while in fact betraying the reputations entrusted to him all over the place:

For the Rogue will speak aloud in the posture of a Whisper; and deny a Woman's name, while he gives you the Marks of her Person: He will forswear receiving a Letter from her, and at the same time, shew you her Hand upon the Superscription: And yet perhaps he has Counterfeited the Hand too; and sworn to a truth; but he hopes not to be believ'd; and refuses the reputation of a Ladies favour, as a Doctor says, No, to a Bishoprick, only that it may be granted him—In short, he is a publick Professor of Secresie, and makes Proclamation that he holds private Intelligence.

(I.i.370—80)

This of course is the crime of crimes in a Restoration gentleman, and stamps Tattle a knave as well as a fool; Congreve takes "that Idol, Reputation" very seriously. Scandal, on the other hand, affects bluntness and plain dealing only the more conveniently to safeguard and protect the reputations of *his* ladies.

Having pursued his pairs of contrasts as far as they will go along this line of development—from courtship through marriage to illicit affairs—Congreve moves on to a more general plane with his pair of fools in *The Way of the World*: Witwoud and Petulant, with their opposed ways of setting up for wit. Witwoud is excessively complaisant and incapable of being offended, since he construes any insult as "raillery." Yet—somewhat like Tattle, in another area—he will imply that an absent friend is stupid and inferior as soon as he gets a chance, while all the time protesting his own good nature and undying friendship. Petulant is all offensiveness and "severity": "When you have made a handsome Woman blush," says Mirabell, "then you think you have been severe."

Of course there are more central and significant contrasts than these to be found in Congreve's comedies—Mirabell versus Fainall, for example—but I have not picked out the above at random: they are the contrasting parallels which Congreve himself has chosen to emphasize. They are set up very deliberately, and "serve as a basis of composition": many scenes are entirely built on them, and they are some of Congreve's funniest scenes. The insistence on the contrast and parallelism of these follies—understandable as a device of composition—is a little irritating sometimes, and suggests "humours" characters. But it is definitely not a question of displaying deplorable opposites and recommending a golden mean between them. If this were didactic satire, it would be completely unhelpful; for where would a golden mean between Scandal and Tattle lie, or between Vainlove and Bellmour? For all the exaggerated symmetry of their deployment, these are psychological studies. Vainlove is true to life: it is true, and a real problem (which exercises Millamant a great deal) that "fondness" is not attractive, not exciting. However regrettable, it is a fact of human nature, as are the hypocrisies of a Tattle and a Witwoud. Congreve's Vainloves are not satire, but a mapping of the pattern that *is there*, the pattern of human relationships in society; such characters are preliminaries to a solution of how to live *in* the pattern, not of how to idealize oneself out of it. Congreve is distinguished by his constant awareness of basic appetites and needs, especially sexual, physical and emotional needs, seeking an outlet in the real world of social life. The Beaumont and Fletcher posturing in which the man alternately adores his mistress and stabs her (as in *Phylaster* and *The Faithful Shepherdess*) will not do, and the Elizabethan dinging of wedding bells after pastoral symbolic trials will not do either: marriage is a serious and chancy business. Through Vainloves and Bellmours, Scandals and Tattles, Congreve works towards his answer in Mirabell and Millamant, who playfully adopt pretence, making a serious game of it, thus allowing delicacy and passion: an artistically expressed and enjoyed passion. To make this possible, however, the drains of the house have to be in order, and Mirabell spends much of his time prudently making sure that they are (the marrying of his servant, the placing in trust of

Mrs. Fainall's estate, and so on). Fainall and Mrs. Marwood lack his self-control in emotional relationships and his moderate degree of prudent benevolence. It is a question of art for life's sake, and they are constantly spoiling the work of art of their lives at critical moments. Life lived with art, however, gives the maximum degree of satisfaction obtainable in the circumstances of human life. It is not out of character that Congreve should have insisted on being approached as a gentleman rather than a writer by Voltaire: the proof of literature lay in the quality of life it induced.

All this is foreshadowed by the delicate undercutting of posturing in *Incognita*, a posturing which the characters themselves are too young not to take seriously. In *Incognita*, Congreve is already working on a special, limited aspect of the problem of the good life: he is testing the "tidy" patterns offered by romantic literature, and finding that they will not, eventually, do, although they do have value.

VII. Conclusion

The style of Congreve's *Incognita* is "self-conscious," intrusive, talkative: he frequently addresses the reader, anticipates his criticisms, and teases him. This way of writing was a natural choice for a young beginner, since it was highly fashionable in the Restoration period (by which I understand the period 1660—1700, as is usually done in the phrase "Restoration comedy"), and particularly in the 1690's. Congreve's best and most characteristic manner is achieved, not by mere chattiness and reader-baiting, but by a fragmentary parody of contemporary narrative technique, especially of the early attempts at realism of for example Aphra Behn.

His subject is superficially a poor match for his style: it is a traditional, romantic, very neat and symmetrical story. Actually, however, Congreve's treatment of this story makes it fit his "facetious" manner excellently: for by subtly exaggerating and underlining its very traditionalness and neatness, *Incognita* parodies its own structure, and embodies in itself an awareness of the inadequacy of its own conventions. It is not a travesty, as literary parody in the Restoration period usually tended to be, but an affectionate, sympathetic parody.

Congreve shows in *Incognita* the same attitude to the literary clichés of his time—the "plotty" love story with its mistaken identities and its happy ending, the ineffectual heroic attitude, the "scrupulous" Restoration heroine, the obligatory tournament—as he was later to display towards the finest human characters in his own comedies. He is interested in exploring and playing with the conventions available to him, just as he later explores and plays with ideas about human relationships and society in his plays. In *Incognita*, the result of his playful testing is finally negative: there is nothing in these literary attitudes that will really do, although at the same time they do have an emotional and aesthetic value; consequently, *Incognita* both ridicules and cherishes these things. It is Congreve's farewell, not only to prose fiction, but to the hope of finding liveable, practicable human and particularly sexual relations in the idealized conceptions of love in the romantic literary tradition. He was really interested in the relevance of literature to life; and consequently he turned to the drama, where, in spite of the "plotty" plots which the contemporary comedy form demanded, he could far more effectively portray and explore relatively realistic relationships, conditioned by the society in which he lived.

I believe, then, that the writing of *Incognita* was, for Congreve, a necessary preliminary exploration of the patterns of romantic literature, before he turned to the exploration of the patterns of contemporary life; a labour for which he could find a model in the plays of Etherege. To read *Incognita* is not only an enjoyable experience—and I hope I have conveyed some of my own enjoyment of it in this thesis—but also an exercise which deepens the enjoyment and understanding of Congreve's comedies.

Appendix: "The Preface to the Reader"

Irène Simon writes that "Congreve's Preface to *Incognita* is the first important document in the criticism of fiction and foreshadows Fielding's classic Preface."[1] In a footnote to this sentence, she justifies its implied dismissal of the earlier discussions of fiction in the prefaces to romances by quoting Charles Davies' statement that romance prefaces such as Roger Boyle's, George Mackenzie's and Robert Boyle's "occupy a place in the long argument about Romance somewhat apart from the development which preceded the emergence of the novel proper in eighteenth-century England."[2] This distinction seems arbitrary: Congreve's Preface is steeped in awareness of the long argument about romance.

Simon describes three points made by Congreve in the Preface:

(1) He has imitated dramatic writing in observing the "unities" more strictly than had been done before, especially in having the obstacles conduce to the end.

(2) He distinguishes the novel as more familiar and credible than the miraculous and incredible romances.

(3) He suggests that novels are related to romances as comedies to tragedies.

At the same time, she points out that French critics insisted on the episodes being contributive to the main design, which is surely the only "unity" worth bothering with; that (2) was altogether a commonplace; and that (3) is thrown off without being developed in any way, nor inspiring any later writers.

Point (2) has interested literary historians; but Congreve's distinction between novels and romances is hardly the pioneering contribution to the theory of the novel which it might seem. If we discount his use of the term "novel" for a moment, and if we do take "the long argument about Romance" into account, then Congreve is really only making the same claim for his book as the romance-writers were always making for theirs. To complain about those who "can relish no Romance that is not forced with extravagant impossibili-

---

[1] "Early Theories of Prose Fiction: Congreve and Fielding," in *Imagined Worlds: Essays on Some English Novels and Novelists in Honour of John Butt*, ed. Maynard Mack and Ian Gregor (London, 1968), p. 19.

[2] *Prefaces to Four Seventeenth-Century Romances*, Augustan Reprint Society, No. 42 (1953), Introduction, p. 1.

ties,"[3] not to mention those whose episodes are no necessary part of the whole, and to assure the reader that *this* work is altogether more realistic and well-constructed, was almost obligatory if one wished to write a preface at all (cf. II:ii above).

Moreover, Congreve's terminology was not new either. Segrais had distinguished the *nouvelle* as more *vraisemblable* than the *roman* as early as 1656, although the unrealistic feature of the *roman* that he was concerned with was not the extravagant adventures of the heroic romance, but instead the extravagant and unrealistic demands for *bienséance* of the *roman d'amour*. His *Les Nouvelles françoises: ou Les Divertissemens de la princesse Aurelie* (Paris, 1656—57) is a "framed" collection of tales: the Princess Aurelie and her courtly friends tell each other stories, and criticize each other's contributions. It is in one of these "frame" discussions that the Princess defines the difference between *roman* and *nouvelle,* in order to meet the various criticisms made by the company of the story she has just told them. These criticisms centre upon offences against *les beaux sentiments*, and may be paraphrased as "it may be *vraisemblable* but it is not nice." That a man should fall in love with his best friend's wife, as happens in the story, is admittedly the sort of thing that happens in real life, but

> cela n'empesche pas, dit Silerite, que ce manquement de foy ne soit contre les beaux sentimens, et vous sçavez que dans les Romans, il ne faut pas faire ny dire rien qui y déroge. (pp. 234—35)

The whole conversation, with its fine-drawn investigation of who in the story is blameable and why, is very much of the *ruelle*. The scruples of morals and of fittingness (the latter include the question whether a German hero who has to dress like a girl at one point ought not to be represented as being of some other nation, "car il me semble qu'un Alleman deguisé en fille est quelque chose de bien extraordinaire") are elegantly evaded by the Princess' distinction, which rescues fiction from dying of an overdose of decorum by abandoning the term to which the criticisms attached, *roman*:

> Ie n'aurois qu'à vous répondre à toutes deux que nous auons entrepris de raconter les choses comme elles sont, & non pas comme elles doiuent estre: Qu'au reste il me semble que c'est la difference qu'il y a entre le Roman, & la Nouuelle, que le Roman écrit ces choses comme la bien-sceance le veut & à la maniere du Poëte; mais que la nouuelle doit un peu dauantage tenir de l'histoire & s'attacher plustost à donner les images des choses comme d'ordinaire nous les voyons arriuer, que comme nostre imagination se les figure. (pp. 240—41)

This, admittedly, is no central part of either the theory or practice of Segrais himself: he is otherwise very keen on *la bienséance*.

---

[3] Ibid., p. ii; Davies is quoting John Bulteel, *Preface to Birinthea* (1664).

When the three points made in Congreve's Preface are viewed in the context of contemporary discussion, then, not much seems to remain of the "important document." Simon admits, as I pointed out above, that the theoretical dicta of the Preface are not very original, and she arrives at an assessment of its significance which is rather more modest than her opening claims suggest:

> The interest of the Preface lies not so much in Congreve's preference for matter nearer to reality as in the confession of the pains he took in the composition of the story. His novel is a delightful arabesque, and the chief merit of the Preface is to have insisted on the need for form, or at least for clever contrivance, in fiction as in the other arts. (p. 23)

This is true, I think. At the same time, it should be noted that Congreve's Preface is all of a piece with the rest of *Incognita*: the playful voice of the narrator is heard here too. The passage where he speaks about "taking pains" is strongly reminiscent of the passage in *Incognita* proper where he ponders whether or not it is worth while apologizing to the reader (cf. III:iii above):

> Some authors are so fond of a Preface, that they will write one tho' there be nothing more in it than an Apology for its self. But to show thee that I am not one of those, I will make no Apology for this, but do tell thee that I think it necessary to be prefix'd to this Trifle, to prevent thy overlooking some little pains which I have taken in the Composition of the following Story. (p. 32)

This is at least doubtful in tone. At the end of the Preface Congreve does apologize for "its self," admitting that it would have been "more proper" for the reader to have been left to find out the beauties Congreve has been describing for himself, from the book itself; and he affects merely to have "gratified the Bookseller in pretending an occasion for a Preface" (p. 34).

All this self-protective irony does not, however, entirely nullify the assured and matter-of-fact tone in which Congreve, in the central part of his Preface, makes the three points which I described above; they are not very original, but they are made with a confidence which is in strong contrast to the apologetic tone in which the romance-writers usually attempted to defend their work.[4] He *has* indeed taken pains, and with a worthy project, he implies. Since this is so, his "modest" disclaimer at the end (". . . an Essay began and finished in the idler hours of a fortnight's time: for I can only esteem it a laborious idleness, which is Parent to so inconsiderable a Birth") seems not only transparently untrue but peculiarly inappropriate. This kind of disclaimer was such a matter of course that it was liable to be stuck on as an afterthought to the most uninhibited boasting about how *much* care the author

---

[4] See Magendie, *Le Roman français*, pp. 123–5, and compare the *Prefaces to Four Seventeenth-Century Romances*, passim.

had lavished on the work. Dryden effortlessly mingles the pen worn to the quill with the trifle of an idle hour in his prefaces, and earlier in the century Charles Sorel, whose preface to *Francion* (1623) outdoes Dryden in self-praise and claims to the highest motives of improving mankind, interlards these with equally proud claims to have written merely for his own amusement and being half asleep half the time anyway. The surprising thing about Sorel is that he comes out and *says* what all the others merely imply:

Il est donc aysé a cognoistre par la negligence que j'advoue selon ma sincerité conscentieuse quel rang pourront tenir justement les ouvrages où sans m'espargner je voudray porter mon esprit a ses extremes efforts.[5]

As fas as I can make out, he is being perfectly serious. The romance-writers excelled in this kind of modesty; but writers in other genres, who were not ashamed of their form, excused their own performance in the same way. Congreve is, I think, only half ironic in his conformism to custom here. The affectation had to wait for Swift to be murdered as it deserved:

I here present *Your Highness* with the Fruits of a very few leisure Hours, stollen from the short Intervals of a World of Business, and of an Employment quite alien from such Amusements as this: The poor Production of that Refuse of Time which has lain heavy upon my Hands, during a long Prorogation of Parliament, a great Dearth of Forein News, and a tedious Fit of rainy Weather.[6]

---

[5] *Romanciers du XVIIe siècle*, ed. Antoine Adam (Paris, 1958), p. 63.
[6] *A Tale of a Tub*, ed. A. C. Guthkelch and D. Nichol Smith (1920; rpt. Oxford, 1958), p. 30.

Bibliography

This is not a bibliography of works useful for the study of Congreve's *Incognita*, but merely a list of works quoted or referred to in this thesis. It lists only those editions to which I have had direct access; that is, it does not include, for instance, such early texts as I quote via a secondary source.

i. Editions of *Incognita*

"Incognita." An abridged edition by "the most ingenious Corinna," in Charles Wilson [Esq., pseud.], *Memoirs of the Life, Writings, and Amours of William Congreve Esq.* (London, 1730), Pt. 2, pp. 70—124.
Incognita. Ed. H. F. B. Brett-Smith. The Percy Reprints, No. 5. Oxford, 1922.
The Complete Works of William Congreve, I. Ed. Montague Summers. 1924; reissued (limited ed.) New York, 1964.
"Incognita" and "The Way of the World." Ed. A. Norman Jeffares. London, 1966.

ii. Other Primary Sources

An Account of the Ceremonies Observed at the Coronation of the Kings and Queens of England. London, [1727] (British Museum Library).
Behn, Aphra. *The Works of Aphra Behn.* Ed. Montague Summers. 6 vols. London, 1915.
Boileau-Despréaux, Nicolas. *Œuvres complètes.* Ed. Charles-H. Boudhors. 9 vols. Paris, 1939—52.
Boyle, Roger. *Parthenissa.* London, 1676 (British Museum Library).
[Charleton, Walter.] *The Ephesian Matron.* London, 1659 (British Museum Library).
Congreve, William. *The Complete Plays of William Congreve.* Ed. Herbert Davis. Chicago, 1967.
— *Letters and Documents.* Ed. John C. Hodges. London, 1964.
Critical Essays of the Seventeenth Century. Ed. J. E. Spingarn. 3 vols. Oxford, 1908—09.
Dryden, John. *"Of Dramatic Poesy" and Other Critical Essays.* Ed. George Watson. 2 vols. Everyman's Library, No. 568 and 569. London, 1962.
The Gentleman's Journal: or The Monthly Miscellany. London, 1692—94 (British Museum Library).
Le Pays, Rene. *The Drudge: or The Jealous Extravagant.* London, 1673. A translation of *Zelotyde* (1664): the translator signs himself "J. B." (British Museum Library).

Nashe, Thomas. *The Vnfortvnate Traveller: or The Life of Jacke Wilton.* Ed. H. F. B. Brett-Smith. The Percy Reprints, No. 1. Oxford, 1927.
Pope. Alexander. *The Dunciad.* Ed. James Sutherland. London, 1943. Vol. V of *The Twickenham Edition of the Poems of Alexander Pope*, gen. ed. John Butt.
— *"The Rape of the Lock" and Other Poems.* Ed. Geoffrey Tillotson. 1940; 2nd rev. ed. London, 1954. Vol. II of the above.
Prefaces to Four Seventeenth-Century Romances. Ed. Charles Davies. Publications of the Augustan Reprint Society, No. 42. Los Angeles, 1953.
Restoration Prose Fiction 1600—1700. Ed. Charles C. Mish. Lincoln, 1970.
Scarron, Paul. *Œuvres complètes de Scarron.* Ed. Henri Bénac. 2 vols. Paris, 1951. (The title is misleading, as this contains only the *Roman comique.*)
[Scudéry, Madeleine de.] *Ibrahim: or The Illustrious Bassa. An Excellent New Romance.* Trans. Henry Cogan. London 1652 (British Museum Library).
Segrais, Jean de. *Les Nouvelles françoises: ou Les Divertissemens de la princesse Aurelie.* Paris, 1656—57 (Kungliga Biblioteket, Stockholm).
[Sorel, Charles.] *De la connoissance des bons livres: ou Examen de plusieurs autheurs.* Paris, 1671 (Kungliga Biblioteket, Stockholm).
— *Histoire comique de Francion. Romanciers du XVIIe siècle.* Ed. Antoine Adam. Paris, 1958. Pp. 59—285.
Swift, Jonathan. *"A Tale of a Tub": to Which is Added "The Battle of the Books" and "The Mechanical Operation of the Spirit."* Ed. A. C. Guthkelch and D. Nichol Smith. 1920; 2nd ed. Oxford, 1958.
Villiers, George, Duke of Buckingham. *The Rehearsal.* Ed. Montague Summers. Stratford-upon-Avon, 1914.
Wilson, Charles [Esq., pseud.]. *Memoirs of the Life, Writings, and Amours of William Congreve Esq.* London, 1730 (British Museum Library).

iii. Secondary Sources

Adam, Antoine. *Histoire de la littérature française au XVIIe siècle.* 5 vols. Paris, 1948—56.
Bergson, Henri. *Le Rire: Essai sur la signification du comique.* 1900; 10th ed. Paris, 1913.
Berkeley, David S. "The Art of 'Whining' Love." *SP*, 52 (1955), 478—96.
— *The Précieuse, or Distressed Heroine, of Restoration Comedy.* Oklahoma State University Publications, 56, No. 19. Stillwater, Oklahoma, 1959.
— "*Préciosité* and the Restoration Comedy of Manners." *Huntington Library Quarterly*, 18 (1955), 108—28.
Booth, Wayne C. *The Rhetoric of Fiction.* Chicago, 1961.
— "The Self-Conscious Narrator in Comic Fiction before *Tristram Shandy*." *PMLA*, 67 (1952), 163—85.
Boyce, Benjamin. "The Effect of the Restoration on Prose Fiction." *Tennessee Studies in Literature*, 6 (1961), 77—83.
Crooks, Esther J. "Translations of Cervantes into French." *Cervantes across the Centuries.* Ed. Angel Flores and M. J. Benardete. New York, 1947. Pp. 294—304.
Cunningham, R. N. *Peter Anthony Motteux 1663—1718: A Biographical and Critical Study.* Oxford, 1933.
Dallas, Dorothy. *Le Roman français de 1660 à 1680.* Paris, 1932.

Davis, Walter R. "A Map of Arcadia: Sidney's Romance in Its Tradition." *Sidney's Arcadia*. Yale Studies in English, No. 158. New Haven, 1965. Pp. 1—179.
De Beer, E. S. "Congreve's *Incognita*, the Source of Its Setting, With a Note on Wilson's *Belphegor*." *RES*, 8 (1932), 74—77.
Deloffre, Frédéric. *La Nouvelle en France à l'âge classique*. Paris, 1967.
Dobrée, Bonamy. "Congreve." *Restoration Comedy*. Oxford, 1924. Pp. 121—50. Rpt. *Restoration Drama: Modern Essays in Criticism*. Ed. John Loftis. New York, 1966. Pp. 97—121.
Gosse, Edmund. *Life of William Congreve*. London, 1888.
Haviland, Thomas P. *The Roman de Longue Haleine on English Soil*. Philadelphia, 1931.
Hodges, John C. *The Library of William Congreve*. New York, 1955.
— *William Congreve, the Man*. MLA, General Series, No. 11. New York, 1941.
Knowles, Edwin B. "Cervantes and English Literature." *Cervantes across the Centuries*. Ed. Angel Flores and M. J. Benardete. New York, 1947. Pp. 267—93.
Krohne, Wilhelm. "Congreves Novelle *Incognita*." Diss. Münster, 1924.
Leavis, F. R. "The Irony of Swift." *The Common Pursuit*. 1952; rpt. New York, 1964. Pp. 73—87.
Leavitt, Sturgis E. "Paul Scarron and English Travesty." *SP*, 16 (1919), 108—20.
Leech, Clifford. "Restoration Tragedy: A Reconsideration." *Durham University Journal*, 11 (1950). Rpt. *Restoration Drama: Modern Essays in Criticism*. Ed. John Loftis. New York, 1966. Pp. 144—60.
Levin, Harry. *The Gates of Horn: A Study of Five French Realists*. New York, 1966.
Lubbock, Percy. *The Craft of Fiction*. 1921; rpt. London, 1954.
Lynch, Kathleen M. *The Social Mode of Restoration Comedy*. New York, 1926.
Macaulay, Thomas B. *History of England. The Works*. London, 1873. Vol. I-IV.
Magendie, Maurice. *Le Roman français au XVIIe siècle*. Paris, 1932.
Mish, Charles C. "Best Sellers in Seventeenth-Century Fiction." *Papers of the Bibliographical Society of America*, 47 (1953), 356—73.
— *English Prose Fiction, 1600—1700: A Chronological Checklist*. Mimeograph ed. 1952; 2nd rev. ed. Charlottesville, Virginia, 1967.
— "English Short Fiction in the Seventeenth Century." *Studies in Short Fiction*, 6 (1969), 233—330.
Morgan, Charlotte E. *The Rise of the Novel of Manners: A Study of English Prose Fiction between 1660 and 1740*. Columbia University Studies in English. New York, 1911.
Muscatine, Charles. *Chaucer and the French Tradition: A Study in Style and Meaning*. Berkeley, 1957.
Novak, Maximillian E. "Congreve's *Incognita* and the Art of the Novella." *Criticism*, 11 (1969), 329—42.
Orwell, George [Eric Blair]. "The Art of Donald McGill." *Decline of the English Murder and Other Essays*. Harmondsworth: Penguin Books, 1965. Pp. 142—54.
Palmer, John. *The Comedy of Manners*. London, 1913.
Raleigh, Sir Walter. *The English Novel*. London, 1896.
Schopper, Günter. *Aufbau und Sprache von Congreves "Incognita."* Diss. Mainz, 1967.
Simon, Irène. "Early Theories of Prose Fiction: Congreve and Fielding." *Imagined Worlds: Essays on Some English Novels and Novelists in Honour of John Butt*. Ed. Maynard Mack and Ian Gregor. London, 1968. Pp. 19—35.

Sutherland, James. *English Literature of the Late Seventeenth Century. Oxford History of English Literature.* VI, Oxford, 1969.

Waith, E. M. *The Pattern of Tragicomedy in Beaumont and Fletcher.* Yale Studies in English, No. 120. New Haven, 1952.

Watt, Ian. *The Rise of the Novel: Studies in Defoe, Richardson and Fielding.* 1957; rpt. London: Pelican Books, 1972.

Williams, Aubrey. "Congreve's *Incognita* and the Contrivances of Providence." *Imagined Worlds: Essays on Some English Novels and Novelists in Honour of John Butt.* Ed. Maynard Mack and Ian Gregor. London, 1968. Pp. 3—17.

Wilson, Edward M. "Cervantes and English Literature of the Seventeenth Century." *Bulletin Hispanique*, 50, No. 1 (1948), 27—52.

Wilson, John Harold. "In Petticoat and Breeches." *All the King's Ladies.* Chicago, 1958. Pp. 67—86.

Wolff, Samuel Lee. *The Greek Romances in Elizabethan Prose Fiction.* New York, 1912.

Woodcock, George. *The Incomparable Aphra.* London, 1948.

Wright, Louis B. *Middle-Class Culture in Elizabethan England.* Chapel Hill, N. Carolina, 1935.

Index

Absurdity: in *Incognita*, 49—50; in romances, 63—64
Antithesis, 45—46, 57—58, 62—63. *See also* "Rhetoric"
Arcadia. *See* Sidney, Sir Philip
Beaumont and Fletcher, 70, 71
Behn, Aphra: realism, 24—25, 54, 90; *The Court of the King of Bantam*, 18—19; *The Dumb Virgin*, 76; *The Fair Jilt*, 23—25, 35; *Oroonoko*, 54; *The Unfortunate Bride*, 69—70
Berkeley, David S., 28
Boileau, 79
Booth, Wayne C., 36—37, 39—40
Boyle, Roger, *Parthenissa*, 14, 81
Buckingham, Duke of. *See* Villiers, George
Burlesque, 79—80
Butler, Samuel, *Hudibras*, 34
Cervantes, Miguel de: *Don Quijote*, 16, 54; *Novelas Ejemplares*, 13, 16
Challes, Robert, *Les Illustres Français*, 32
Characterization in *Incognita*, 64, 89
Charleton, Walter, *The Ephesian Matron*, 17, 26
Clothes in *Incognita*, 59—60, 75—77
Conflict between love and duty, friendship, honour, 84—89
Congreve, William: comedies, 89—95 passim; *Memoirs* of (Wilson), 9 n. 3, 91; *The Mourning Bride*, 86—87
Conte, distinguished from *nouvelle*, 13
Corinna, "the ingenious," 9
Court of the King of Bantam, The (Behn), 18—19
Davis, Walter R., 82—83
Defoe, Daniel, *Moll Flanders*, 54
De la connoissance des bons livres (Sorel), 53
Don Quijote (Cervantes), 16, 54
"Dramatick Writing," Congreve's imitation of, 74—77
Dryden, John, *Essay of Dramatic Poesy*, 56

Dumb Virgin, The (Behn), 76
Du Plaisir, *Sentiments sur les lettres et sur l'histoire*, 12, 21—22
Encadrement, 13, 31, 32
Ephesian Matron, The (Charleton), 17, 26
Essay of Dramatic Poesy (Dryden), 56
"Facetious" style, 16—20, 25—46
Fair Jilt, The (Behn), 23—25, 35
"Framed" collections, 13, 31, 32
Gentleman's Journal, The, 19—20, 40
"Histories" inside romances, 29—31, 67
Hudibras (Butler), 34
Ibrahim (Madeleine de Scudéry), 55—56; "histories" in, 67; irony in, 66—68; preface to [Georges de Scudéry], 55—56
Intrusive narrator, 16—40; in Preface, 100
Irony: "dramatic," 57—58, 69, 72; "romantic," 66—68
Journalism, seventeenth-century, 19—20
Le Pays, Rene, *Zelotyde*, 18
Les Illustres Français (Challes), 32
Levin, Harry, 54—55
Local colour in *Incognita*, 46 n. 47, 59
London Spy, The (Ward), 19—20
Lubbock, Percy, 32, 35
Lynch, Kathleen M., 77—78
Memoirs of Congreve (Wilson), 9 n. 3, 91
Mock-heroic, 79—80
Moll Flanders (Defoe), 54
Motteux, Peter, *The Gentleman's Journal*, 19—20, 40
Mourning Bride, The, 86—87
Names, proper, 90
Nashe, Thomas, *The Unfortunate Traveller*, 81, 84
Nouvelle, distinguished from *conte*, 13
Novel: evolution of, 10; "gallant," 12; historical, 12, 31; psychological, 12—13; and romance, distinction between, 12, 15, 98—99. *See also* Prose fiction, seventeenth-century

106

Novelas Ejemplares (Cervantes), 13, 16
Omniscient narrator, 22—36, 68
Oroonoko (Behn), 54
Pamela (Richardson), 62, 63—64
Parody: of realistic devices, 34—35; in the Restoration period, 78—80; of the world of romance, 62—73
Parthenissa (Roger Boyle), 14, 81
Point of view, 22, 29—32
Pope, Alexander, *The Rape of the Lock*, 80
Preface to *Incognita*, 15, 49, 71, 74, 98—101
Proper names, 90
Prose fiction, seventeenth-century: English, 15—20; facetious, 16—36; French, 11—15, 28—33; inconsistent narrative technique in, 22—28; and journalism, 19—20; suspense and surprise in, 69—71. *See also* Novel; Romance
Providence, 57—58
Rape of the Lock, The (Pope), 80
Realism: in Aphra Behn, 24—25, 54, 90; devices of, 29—32. *See also* Levin, Harry; Watt, Ian
Rehearsal, The (Villiers), 79—80, 85—86, 88
Restoration comedy: relation of *Incognita* to, 39, 49, 58, 77—78, 84; "dramatic irony" in, 72; "romantic irony" in, 68
Restoration tragedy, 58, 65—66
"Rhetoric," 35—37, 42—43, 44—46. *See also* Antithesis
Richardson, Samuel, *Pamela*, 62, 63—64
Romance: concept of, 51—55; description in, 61; in England, 14, 53; features of in *Incognita*, 41, 44, 80—88; French seventeenth-century, 11—12, 41, 52—53, 55; Greek, 51—52, 57—58, 71; "histories" in, 29—31, 67; medieval, 52; and novel, distinction between, 12, 15, 98—99; seventeenth-century criticism of, 14—15, 53, 80—81, 98—100

Scarron, Paul, 15—20 passim, 47; novels, 17—18, 40; *Virgile travesti*, 79
Schopper, Günter, 44
Scudéry, Georges de, preface to *Ibrahim*, 55—56
Scudéry, Madeleine de. See *Ibrahim*
Segrais, Jean de: distinction between novel and romance, 15, 99; historical novels, 31
Self-conscious narrator, 36—40
Sentiments sur les lettres et sur l'histoire (Du Plaisir), 12, 21—22
Sidney, Sir Philip, *Arcadia*: antithesis and parallelism, 45—46, 62—63; tidiness, 52; tournaments, 82—83
Simon, Irène, 98—100
Sorel, Charles: *De la connoissance des bons livres*, 53; preface to *Francion*, 101
Style, indivisible from structure, 62—63
Summary: of *Incognita*, 47—49; as ornament, 69
Surprising, the, 69—71. *See also* Antithesis
Suspense, 69—72
Swift, Jonathan, *A Tale of a Tub*, 25, 101
Symmetry. *See* Tidiness
Tale of a Tub, A (Swift), 25, 101
Tidiness: of *Incognita*, 49—50, 55—58, 62—66; of the world of romance, 51—55
Tournament in *Incognita*, 61—62, 80—84
Unfortunate Bride, The (Behn), 69—70
Unfortunate Traveller, The (Nashe), 81, 84
Unity: "of Contrivance," 49—73; of style and structure in *Incognita*, 47, 62—63
Villiers, George, Duke of Buckingham, *The Rehearsal*, 79—80, 85—86, 88
Virgile travesti (Scarron), 79
Ward, Edward, *The London Spy*, 19—20
Watt, Ian, 45, 53—54, 62
Williams, Aubrey, 57—58
Wilson, Charles, *Memoirs*, 9 n. 3, 91
Zelotyde (Le Pays), 18

73

LIBRARY OF DAVIDSON COLLEGE